MIRROR AND MARBLE

MIRROR AND MARBLE

THE POETRY OF
IAIN CRICHTON SMITH

CAROL GOW

LINES REVIEW EDITIONS

SALTIRE

ISBN 0 86334 070 9

Published in 1992 by
The Saltire Society
9 Fountain Close
High Street
Edinburgh EH1 1TF

*The publisher acknowledges
subsidy from the Scottish Arts Council
towards the publication of this volume*

Printed in Scotland by
Macdonald Lindsay Pindar plc
Edgefield Road, Loanhead, Midlothian EH20 9SY

Contents

I—HOME

Ch 1   The Lewis Years   9

II—AWAY

2   The Diamond-Browed One   25

3   Hamlet   51

III—OUTCAST

4   Orpheus   77

5   Crusoe   98

IV—EXILE

6   Oedipus   123

SELECT BIBLIOGRAPHY   155

INDEX   157

I
Home

CHAPTER ONE

The Lewis Years

Iain Crichton Smith has suggested that to be a writer and to be born in Scotland is to be victim of an accident of geography and a hostile history. He is a writer of whom Scotland can be justly proud, yet he has been one of her harshest critics. His writing is deeply rooted in local habitation yet it is of international significance. The Outer Hebridean island of Lewis is arguably the most important influence on his work, yet he left the island at seventeen, never to return to live there. His work is based on such complexities and conflicts: exploring and elucidating them he has produced a body of work which is remarkable in its stubborn pursuit of theme, its rigorous examination of language, its exploration of identity.

Identity is both arbitrary and fixed: accident and fate. Iain Crichton Smith was born in Glasgow on New Year's Day, 1928. The fact is rarely accurately recorded. More commonly, Crichton Smith's biographers refer to his birthplace as the small village of Bayble, on the Outer Hebridean island of Lewis. The error is significant, pointing up neatly the arbitrariness of identity. Crichton Smith's parents, John and Christina Smith, were Lewis-born, but had moved to Glasgow because of John's work as a Merchant Seaman when Iain, their middle son, was born. When Iain was around a year old, John Smith died from tuberculosis. Christina Smith returned to Lewis a widow with three young sons. But if Glasgow was the place of his physical birth, Lewis was the island of Crichton Smith's social birth, his entry into history. Like Mikhail Bakhtin, Crichton Smith's biographers distinguish between a physical and a social birth.[1] They recognise that it is the island of Lewis which gives him everything that is distinctive about his work. No writer can exist outside history: the Lewis background has shaped his work through reaction and resistance. The importance of the Lewis years cannot be underestimated and I offer in the pages of this introduction an account of these first seventeen years which will

9

establish a context for the discussion of the English poetry which follows.

For Iain Crichton Smith, Lewis was "a bare island without theatre, ballet, museums."[2] Discussion of Lewis involves not these institutions of art and culture but instead the institutions of religion and a darker reality of Calvinism, poverty and death. The island in the 1930s and 40s was a Gaelic-speaking community, Calvinist, and relatively classless. In the village of Bayble, everyone knew everyone else, and no-one ever knocked on a door. Crichton Smith describes his boyhood on Lewis in an autobiographical memoir, "Between Sea and Moor," and writes of this period more obliquely in two fictional works: *On The Island*, which portrays the awakening mind of an eleven-year-old Iain, and *The Last Summer*, the story of an adolescent Malcolm living on the island in the 1940s. All three works reveal a sense of displacement and dislocation.

In "Between Sea and Moor" Crichton Smith writes of his past as a lost Eden:

> Days when we played football all day, nights when we played football by the light of the moon, returning home across the moor like sweaty ghosts, the moon a gold football in the sky.
>
> How can one be that boy again? How can one walk home from the well with the two pails brimming with water, on paths that are probably now gone, between the cornfields, and through the long wet grass?[3]

The proleptic "ghosts" in the first paragraph suggests the loss in the second, and also the silence which meets the questions, "how?" This Eden is ghostly perhaps because it was never fully inhabited by the young boy. The childhood picture must include the experience of poverty and frequent ill-health: Crichton Smith's years on Lewis offered him a childhood without luxury and distorted by his mother's fear of tuberculosis.

John Smith's early death meant Christina Smith was left to raise three boys on a widow's pension of around a pound a week. It meant a plain diet: Iain Crichton Smith recalls that he had salt herring and potatoes every day except Sunday.[4] It is a diet which would find much favour with present-day nutritionists, perhaps, but followed out of necessity, not choice. The poverty of his background is best revealed in Crichton Smith's description of an annual day-trip to the main town on the island, Stornoway. By car, today, it is a journey of some twenty minutes. For Crichton Smith, it was a special event, an entry into another world. The delights of Stornoway are likened to the wonders of Babylon; ice cream and apples, books and the cinema delight him and illustrate the complete separation of Babylon and Bayble, similar words which identify separate worlds.[5] The poverty is not only material: the memoir reveals a boy hungry for colour, texture, art.

Ill-health dogged him—prolonged bouts of asthma and bronchitis often kept him away from school. His mother's fear of tuberculosis oppressed him and transmitted itself to him:

> My father had died of TB and my mother was terrified that I would also get the disease, so whenever I coughed I was immediately bundled into bed with hot water-bottles. Sometimes I felt so suffocated by this treatment that whenever I felt a cough coming on I would go into the next room lest she should hear me. . . . Often I would waken at night thinking that I was haemorrhaging, for all around me the village was palpitant with the symptoms of TB of which the young and the middle-aged were dying.[6]

The fear is explored in the novel *The Last Summer*, which Crichton Smith says gives "a certain amount of detail about my childhood and boyhood."[7] His citation of two examples from the novel suggests the horror TB awakened:

> Malcolm would often go and visit Dicky, who had come home from the Army with TB and was dying from it. Malcolm was terrified of TB—of the visible wasting whiteness, like a candle guttering—but nevertheless he forced himself to go. . . . He knew there was a lot of haemorrhaging in TB and in fact Dicky had been taken off the ship in a stretcher, haemorrhaging badly, and this terrified Malcolm so much that one night he had wakened up in the bed beside his brother, feeling that he was being choked by blood. . . .
>
> Malcolm was frightened that Mrs Morrison would offer him tea. He didn't like eating and drinking in the house in case he got germs. For this reason he always came over just after he had had a meal.[8]

The fear is not neurotic, nor was his mother's anxiety groundless. To understand the terror TB aroused it is important to understand its history on the island of Lewis. Tuberculosis was introduced to the island in the latter half of the nineteenth century because many girls left Lewis to work at the herring industry or on the mainland. There, they came into contact with TB germs. They had no natural immunity and so contracted the bacterial disease very easily. In Lewis, the disease was known as *Galair an t-sraingear* (the stranger's disease) and the death rate from it peaked in the first ten years of the twentieth century. The typical "black house" of that period with its thatched roof and smoky atmosphere was a breeding ground for the germs, and overcrowding, an ignorance of precautions, the fact that a family often kept its own cow for milk supply and drank contaminated milk, meant it spread rapidly. The disease was finally conquered by improved housing, the eradication of TB from dairy cattle and the BCG vaccination, but Crichton Smith's boyhood was lived with the very real fear of that disease and its ravages.[9]

Tuberculosis brought home the fact of death early to the growing boy through the death of his father, of friends, of neighbours. The two world wars also provided his island with a history of deaths.

The first world war had seen heavy losses from the island: eight hundred Lewismen were killed in action. But even to an island accustomed to tragedy, the loss of the Admiralty yacht *Iolaire* numbed a community. Returning home on leave on New Year's Eve, two hundred men were drowned when the yacht bringing them home crashed on the rocks known as the Beasts of Holm twenty yards from the shore at 1.55 on New Year's Morning. The tragedy was reported in the *Stornoway Gazette* as a "catastrophe," "the blackest day in the history of the island."[10] The language used half a century later to comment on the event displays shocked disbelief not only at the magnitude of the disaster but at its catastrophic nature; a fate that surely seemed like the vengeance of a wrathful Greek God:

> Every circumstance added to its bitterness—the season of the year; the place where it happened, almost within sight of the pier; the ease of mind people had enjoyed that New Year's Eve believing that the long horror of destruction had ended with the Armistice.
>
> Everyone in Lewis, even those who suffered no personal loss, lived under the shadow of the *Iolaire* for many years. Who of those who saw it will ever forget the little boats working with grappling irons round the rocks at Holm, and the bodies lying in sodden rows on the grass, and the little red and blue country carts coming in from the villages of Barvas, Uig and Lochs, Back and Point, to claim their dead?[11]

Crichton Smith's boyhood was lived under the shadow of the disaster. The experience was to make a deep and lasting impression and if the language used to describe the horror of the event unconsciously created the world of violent grace, the stage of the Greek tragic theatre, Crichton Smith was fully conscious of its nature:

> It has had a deep influence on the way that I think about the world. It is almost a black comedy or a Greek tragedy. I can imagine these people waiting for the ex-servicemen to come home, with lamps lit, food on the table and so on. And then they are drowned. And this in an island which was religious and still of course is. I cannot imagine what that tragedy must have done to those people, to Lewis. In fact it is said that one widow's son was washed up at her door after serving four years in France. It all looks like a macabre joke.[12]

In contrast, the second world war seemed less real. The tragedy was enacted off-stage. No bombs fell on Lewis, and life seemed little different—except that the boys and men of the village left to join the Navy, many of them to go down with their ships. There was a sense that the malign deity was still at work, insidiously, invisibly. Villages would gather in the house which had a battery-operated radio and hear news of ships that had been sunk, losses that had been sustained. More distanced from the tragedy, the effects of the second world war were nevertheless felt by the islanders in the loss from the community of the able-bodied men and boys who went to fight. The village became a community of children, women and the old.

What comfort did the Calvinist religion offer those who endured these wars? Perhaps little. The Calvinism of the island was a harsh, strict creed. Crichton Smith's description of his island as lacking theatre and ballet is significant: Calvinism taught that art, music and dance were dangerous follies which led to hell and damnation. Crichton Smith recalls an incident from his past which is illuminating here. One day, his mother found him carving little wooden hens. She remarked impatiently, "Why do you make wooden hens when the Lord has made real ones?"[13] Such acts created graven images.

During Crichton Smith's formative years, the phenomenon of "swooning" swept the island, an event which for many recalled the great religious revival of 1859, the *Bliadhna an Aomaidh*, the year of the swooning.[14] Swooning involved such manifestations as cries, paralysis, jerking limbs and spasms. Evening church meetings would begin at ten. At midnight, as many as forty or fifty of the congregation would crowd into a private house and continue the prayer meeting for two or three hours. In this intense atmosphere, many would rise spontaneously to pray, interrupting psalms. As emotion heightened, many would call out in Gaelic to relatives, weeping. Others collapsed, apparently paralysed, and would have to be carried out to recover.[15]

The power of the church was felt in other ways too, and is felt, many suggest, even today. Recently, Caledonian MacBrayne's decision to operate Sunday ferry services to the island ran into a "'Hebridean hurricane' of opposition from the defiant Sabbatarians on the Isle of Lewis." Angus Smith, the Free Church Minister who led a battle to block Sunday services to Skye in 1967, took a leading part in the protest. Many islanders welcomed the new service, but were afraid to speak up, one local businessman claimed, because of a "climate of intimidation" on the island: the church controlled the local council which was a big employer. Those who ran hotels, bars, shops or taxi services were under constant pressure.[16]

Crichton Smith's own experience recognises such pressures. He sees his Calvinist inheritance in negative terms:

I think I feel it more and more strongly now the older I grow that it has done harm. . . . I feel it has done harm to my own psychology—this kind of—this kind of depressive lack of joy . . . this kind of uniformity.[17]

He is aware of the benefits of community, but clearly defines the pressure on the individual:

The idea of honour or fame, as concerning above all individual achievement unrelated to community, was not a worthwhile one. Those who had *cliù* were those who conformed to the *mores* of the society and its ideals. The film star who has a high reputation but is morally tainted would not in such a society have *cliù*. The moral parameters were inextricably intertwined with the social ones.[18]

To be a poet, then, was to set oneself apart. To write in English meant a double indictment: "For the islander to be influenced by T. S. Eliot or William Carlos Williams instead of Duncan Ban Macintyre is almost to be a traitor."[19]

The Lewis of Crichton Smith's social birth was therefore an island where the experience of poverty was gained early, where the fact of death was part of a personal and community history, where religion gave little comfort and taught sobriety, discipline—and above all the importance of community over the individual. The Lewis childhood then is the background which forms the poet and yet Crichton Smith's comment below reveals that child as a stranger now to himself:

I think I was really a very isolated child, isolated in school and perhaps in the village too. . . . I lived in a state of perpetual humiliation, shy and secretive, often ill, and when I look at the class photograph that was taken then . . . I see a child whose eyes are heavy and almost dim with fright, staring into a world which he finds threatening.[20]

The child is also stranger to his community, an outsider. He stares "into" a world which seems hostile. Set apart, he is the observer.

Crichton Smith's experience of Lewis offers a sombre picture: an island without culture, and described in terms of its religion, its history of deaths, and poverty. There are many who would challenge that view. Professor Derick Thomson was also raised on the island, in the village of Bayble, and was, in fact, a friend of Crichton Smith's older brother. If the title of Crichton Smith's memoir, "Between Sea and Moor," reveals the conflicts he experienced, the title of Professor Thomson's companion essay, "A Man Reared in Lewis," suggests an identity rooted firmly in history. Professor Thomson's memoir presents a different picture of Lewis. His father was the local schoolmaster and he was raised in a bilingual household. English was his first language.

> I think this was a carefully worked-out policy, for we were in the midst of an almost totally Gaelic environment, and they reckoned that Gaelic would come easily.

His memoir sets down a history, recording a

> small nexus of Thomson families in Tong, as also in neighbouring villages, and another in Ness, all deriving from a common ancestor, a James Thomson (the same name as my father) from Speyside who had come to Lewis in 1737 as a teacher for the Society for the Propagation of Christian Knowledge.[21]

Such differences can account for different experiences. Professor Thomson suggests that Crichton Smith's definition of culture is revealing:

> He thought there was no "culture" in Bayble. This is largely a matter of definition. Of course he had a point, but it was too narrow a view, arrogant and lacking in understanding.[22]

Contrasting his own upbringing on the island with Crichton Smith's, he is sensitive to the reasons for their different views:

> He didn't have a very secure family background in a way—father dead, probably very short of cash, not very fully integrated into the village, to which they had come from Glasgow. By contrast, my father was the local schoolmaster, and a prominent Gaelic activist and writer, and my mother was also very interested in Gaelic poetry and song. It was perhaps easier for Iain to see a specific identity in what came his way of current fashionable English literature (and there was, after all, nothing remotely comparable in Gaelic at the time—no literary periodicals, scarcely any new books).[23]

The Lewis of Crichton Smith's poetry, then, is not the Lewis Derick Thomson experienced. Nor is it the misty Hebridean island glorified in songs and poems of exile. Crichton Smith's confrontational and negative attitude towards his Gaelic culture is not the only stance which can produce fine poetry, but in his case it has produced a writer whose poetry must be ranked in the first order. The Lewis background is seen by Crichton Smith as hostile to his art: a source of opposition, threat, the negation of his poetry, whose embodiment is the old woman, the face of Calvinism.

Derick Thomson was fortunate in that he was brought up with a knowledge of Gaelic culture. If Crichton Smith perceived the island as lacking culture, the lack he senses is created by, and begins to be filled by, the education system. For the young, alienated boy, entry into education meant entry into the English language and its literary riches, and, as Professor Thomson suggests, the embracing of an identity which set him apart from his background.

Unlike Derick Thomson, for the first five years of his life, Crichton Smith lived in a wholly Gaelic world: he and his friends, his family and their neighbours, spoke only Gaelic. When he was five years old, he walked through the doors of the Bayble primary school and straight into an English world. In 1933, a child could be punished for speaking Gaelic in the playground. English was the language of education: all lessons were in English, although Gaelic was often taught as a subject, much the way that French, German or other "foreign" languages are taught nowadays. Crichton Smith has said he cannot remember now how he achieved the transition from Gaelic to English. He does suggest the experience is a "blow to the psyche, an insult to the brain" and might be "a classic recipe for schizophrenia."[24] It is probable his experience was similar to the experience of Harris-born writer Finlay J. Macdonald, who writes of his first day at school in metaphors which insist on the break with the Gaelic world. The loosing of his father's hand, the delivery of his brand-new suited self to the care of Miss Dalbeith, is a scarring experience. The realisation that they inhabit two different worlds, Gaelic and English, comes quickly:

> While I had enough Gaelic to last me for the rest of my life, she didn't have a word of Gaelic in her head.
> I would willingly have solved the language problem for her by slipping off home—but she was a resourceful woman. She led me by the forelock to the end of a five-seater desk where there was an empty seat beside a girl. She patted the wooden seat first, and then mine. She said "sit" and pressed me down hard, and so I learned my first word of English as if I were being groomed for Crufts.[25]

Crichton Smith has no such recollection of that moment of entry into an English world. Perhaps that in itself is significant. Finlay J. Macdonald writes of the loosing of his father's hand: behind him is a family, a community, in which he feels at home. Crichton Smith's sense of alienation means that, for him, the break with community offers not separation but escape, the discovery of an identity and a home. Certainly he seems to have embraced the "Englishness" into which he was catapulted. In *The Last Summer*, school beckons like Eden:

> How long ago that seemed! Running barefoot to school while the headmaster waited with the whistle in his mouth and you ran like the wind and the iron bell clanged and the strawberries were growing

in the garden and the teachers—all women—were waiting to welcome you into their huge arms and bosoms and the walls were bright with all the maps of the world.[26]

The parallel construction, "while," "and," "and," throws into relief the parenthetical "all women" which, in the context, strains to become "all woman." Set the language of this prose with its bright maps, bosoms, huge arms and strawberries against the old woman of Crichton Smith's poetry whose "set mouth / forgives no one" or the "Face of An Old Highland Woman," with "two eyes like lochs staring up / from heather gnarled by a bare wind" and you set against a harsh Calvinism an idyllic world of learning, against the black matriarch a sensuous, buxom mistress.[27] These are the two homes, the two worlds, in which the growing boy is offered a place, an identity.

Though Crichton Smith has used the phrase "between two worlds" to describe his position, and speaks of being forced to choose, it seems clear that the world of his English education offered him a home in which he could flourish, an identity which he sought. The chronic bouts of asthma and bronchitis which troubled him throughout his boyhood cleared up completely when he left Lewis to begin studying at Aberdeen. Revealed in the comparison between the prose passage and the two poems is the contrast between the stuff of life and the stuff of death.

Not unusually, his academic career pushed him relentlessly away from his community. At eleven he won a scholarship to the Nicolson Institute in Stornoway, the "Babylon" of his early childhood, leaving behind many of his former schoolmates who did not make the journey into town. The loosing of the father's hand which Finlay J. Macdonald describes is the perfect metaphor for the education system, then. The severing of the Gaelic child from his community was an inevitability. With hindsight, Crichton Smith expresses concern at this path:

> Though I was learning geometry and Latin, and enjoying doing so, I was also losing something precious which I feel I ought not to have been forced to lose.
>
> I can't say that I would have expressed my confused feelings so clearly then but I did have a dim intuition that there was something wrong, that I was being relentlessly forced to choose between two worlds.[28]

Two worlds: Bayble and Stornoway, Gaelic and English. Stornoway, with its neat streets, shops and trees, was the place where he gained his classic English education, where he inhabited an English world. If his English education was embraced willlingly, innocently, conflicts did begin to emerge. In retrospect, Iain Crichton Smith is able to bring these conflicts into sharper focus:

17

It seems to me that there ought to have been some way in which I did not have to be processed into an English system, in which the dichotomy between Gaelic and English did not have to be so sharp and merciless. I feel that we ought to have been taught through the medium of Gaelic (at least in my early years) and allowed to retain that communal wholeness which is so important.[29]

Communal wholeness: an Edenic view of the past? Real or imagined, it is fractured by Crichton Smith's education, both formal and informal. His boyhood reading also catapulted him into an English world. The poetry of Keats, Shelley and Kipling, the novels of P. C. Wren and Dickens, pulp detective stories and westerns, *Chambers Journal*, children's comics—these offered him a language, an identity, a world. Small wonder that the poems of his youth reflected not the world around him but the world of his reading. He wrote in the style of Keats and Shelley and "sometimes in the style of Sir Walter Scott." At eighteen, embarked on a university education in which English authors predominated, he wrote a poem called, with some significance, "Bookworm," which is "composed I think of an Eliotish obscurity combined at the end with a certain simplicity."[30]

Leaving for Aberdeen brought relief. Crichton Smith no longer felt torn between two worlds, no longer felt a stranger in his island because in Aberdeen he achieved a sense of freedom, a sense of anonymity: "I was happier because I didn't carry daily on my shoulders the weight of a village tradition and the style of the *Aeneid*."[31] His experience seemed to be one of liberation, not loss. Among his friends at Aberdeen University in 1945 were Alexander Scott, Derick Thomson and Kenneth Buthlay. Here, then, he seemed to have found a home, the company of others who wrote poetry. Yet what Crichton Smith describes as a "key incident" in his life reveals that the escape was not so clean. No-one who listens to Crichton Smith speak, or who reads the poetry or the prose, can escape for long the story of the blind beggar.[32] Stepping off the train in Aberdeen for the first time, the seventeen-year-old saw a blind beggar in black glasses on the platform. "Saw" is perhaps the wrong word here: "was confronted by" or "was subjected to that blind gaze" perhaps points towards a fuller explanation of why this incident should be so persistently and stubbornly analysed. The seventeen-year-old was no doubt confused and embarrassed by the sudden clash of two cultures: in Lewis, such a man would have been cared for by the community. But the blind gaze of that beggar has maintained its significance for him perhaps because it has the power of the blind gaze of Teiresias, the blind seer who confronts Oedipus and forces the question "who am I?" To be a young man, away from home in an environment of books and

18

learning, may have seemed like a fresh start, a new life, but his reaction to that beggar reveals the claim of his social birth, his formative years, and foregrounds disjunction: it is that disjunction which is constantly explored in the poetry and offers him a distinctive voice.

The self is perceived in two mirrors; a Gaelic, Calvinistic culture and an English culture of learning and books. The twin poles of his art are beautifully captured in an image from *The Last Summer*:

> Shifting a bit, Malcolm looked sideways and noticed for the first time that the bible was lying on top of a Penguin *New Writing*.[33]

Perspective is foregrounded in the quotation and is an important concept in Crichton Smith's work. It is sufficient to note here, however, that the quotation reveals choice cannot be made cleanly. Identity is overlaid, fragmented. The image of the Bible lying on top of a book of poetry suggests the weight of the Gaelic inheritance.

The mirror is an important image in the poetry: the distorted image in the glass, the face in the spoon. I have already made use of Bakhtin's idea of a double birth; a physical birth and a historical birth, the latter the entry into a culture and an identity. The psychologist Jacques Lacan's theories about this social birth have been fruitful to literary critics: he suggests that fragmentation occurs at this moment of social birth, the entry into identity. The child of around eighteen months who begins to achieve a sense of self by seeing that self reflected back to it by its community is deceived. The reflection offers not wholeness but alienation and fragmentation. Lacan writes of the Self and the Other, foregrounding the disjunction between the individual and the Other, the self perceived in the mirror of society which seems to offer a fragmented self wholeness, unity—an identity. Lacan's theories and their usefulness as tools for the literary critic of Crichton Smith's work are outside the scope of this book but the reader who wishes to pursue such connections will find them fruitful.[34] It is sufficient to note here that the child who is reared in a society with a strong sense of community and who yet perceives his position as the misfit perceives a distorted image in the glass. Crichton Smith's experience makes him aware of the disjunction between Self and Other. A sense of wholeness is provided neither by the mirror of his Gaelic society, nor his world of English education. His identity is fragmented.

The following chapters will explore the discourse of the "I" in Crichton Smith's poetry and establish a pattern of dispossession. Each "I," an established identity and a language, is discarded as if in a search for some sovereign territory. Each "I" is found to be, in Crichton Smith's own metaphor, "a shabby skin": a skin because it offers wholeness and identity; shabby because he ruthlessly exposes it as a shabby lie and also because it is worn out, exhausted, and can no longer contain the exploration of identity. In the novel *My Last Duchess*, the hero's damning verdict on himself is that he is "homo textual."[35] To accept that is to accept identity as a construction of language.

The "I" of Crichton Smith's poetry works to find sovereign territory—and the interlocutor in Crichton Smith's work is always a woman in a black dress, a man in a black hat, the threatening figures from his background who oppress, deny, and silently judge. It is against this claim of his background that Crichton Smith posits his "I." Always there is a doubt that such opposition is not outside at all, but lies deep within. The metaphors Crichton Smith used in 1963 to describe the development of his poetry were metaphors of surface and depths: "The thing is to drill down, where one meets with the same people, though at the top they may appear to be different."[36] Exploring the depth of self, the poet fears the discovery that he, too, may be the same: that the Calvinist Gael, the bourgeois Scot, is the ultimate reflection which awaits him.

The following chapters offer the narrative of Crichton Smith's poetry. I will trace a development which seems to lead him away from his origins but which unexpectedly threatens to lead him home, to inscribe him son. The pattern can be traced in the imagery he uses to describe his poetry. In the early stages, he uses the metaphor of a brimming vase. Later, he returns to the image of the well from the early "Poem of Lewis" and his childhood idyll, "Between Sea and Moor": writing poetry is like carrying a bucket home from the well, careful not to spill a drop.[37] The development of the imagery is a useful aid to understanding the development I will trace in the following chapters. Against the deep well he sets a brimming vase, the creation of an "I" and a language in opposition to his background. The well is a metaphor for the source of commuity. It is a practical, functional container. The vase is a metaphor for the poem as aesthetic object. The evolution of the bucket image is complex: the poetic vase becomes prosaic bucket; the brimming vase, suggesting surplus, becomes the full bucket, carried carefully so as not to spill a drop. And the vase once used as an image to set against the deep well becomes the bucket which is used to draw from that deep source. Such a development suggests a poet honing his language, working towards a relationship with his Gaelic inheritance and attempting to admit it into his work as an antithetical testing force which is also a means of balance.

I will trace three movements; away, isolation, exile. I will show that Crichton Smith's poetry is a poetry of exploration and testing. In 1986, Crichton Smith wrote

I recall with a sense of injustice my own fragmented life, the choices

I had to make when I didn't realise that I was making them, the losses I endured before I well knew that I was enduring them, the contradictions I was involved in before I knew they existed. And I know that my own life has been a snake pit of contradictions, because of an accident of geography and a hostile history. I envy, for instance, those poets who have developed in a stable society, who can start from there and are not constantly analysing the very bases of their art.[38]

The quotation reveals a sense of loss, perceived in a backward glance, when it is too late. It is never too late for the poet to account for that loss. The finality of a statement like "I have made the choice. I have forsaken the community in order to individualise myself" belies the problem of the guilt that accompanies the freedom, the loss that is the obverse of gain.[39] Crichton Smith's poetry offers not a solution to these problems, but an elucidation and a clarification.

It is not my purpose to evaluate the poetry. Iain Crichton Smith has been well served by contemporary reviewers and there are several excellent short critical studies available. This book addresses itself to the need for an overview of Iain Crichton Smith's work, one which reveals not the merit of individual poems or volumes but which reveals the remarkable unity of the whole *oeuvre*. I offer in the following pages an account which allows the reader to perceive Crichton Smith's work as a continuous and continuing narrative. Although I make reference to Gaelic poems in translation by Crichton Smith where pertinent, the narrative is traced through the poems written in English, from 1955-1992.

Notes

1. Tzevetan Todorov, *Mikhail Bakhtin: The Dialogical Principle*, translated by Wlad Godzich (Manchester: Manchester University Press, 1984), p. 31.
2. "Between Sea and Moor," in *As I Remember*, edited by Maurice Lindsay (London: Hale, 1979), pp. 107-121 (p. 115).
3. *Ibid.*, pp. 108-9.
4. John Blackburn, "A Writer's Journey," booklet and five cassette recordings (Edinburgh: Moray House College of Education, 1981).
5. *As I Remember*, p. 110.
6. *Ibid.*, p. 111.
7. "The Highland Element In My English Work," *Scottish Literary Journal*, 4 (1977), 47-60 (p. 49).
8. *The Last Summer* (London: Gollancz, 1969), p. 34; p. 35.
9. John M. MacLeod, "Social and Economic Conditions in Lewis," *Eilean An Fhraoich Annual* (December 1977), 13-21.
10. *Sea Sorrow* (Stornoway: *Gazette*, 1972), p. 5.
11. *Ibid.*, p. 2.
12. "The Highland Element In My English Work," p. 51.
13. John Blackburn, "A Writer's Journey."

14. Iain H. Murray (editor), *The Diary of Kenneth MacRae* (Edinburgh: The Banner of Truth Trust, 1980), p. 366.
15. *Ibid.*, p. 365.
16. Frazer Grigor, "Sunday Grip On Island Weakens," *Sunday Times*, 25 September 1988, p. A5.
17. Interview with Iain Crichton Smith, Taynuilt, 1987.
18. "Real People in a Real Place," in *Towards the Human* (Edinburgh: Macdonald, 1986), pp. 13-70 (p. 44).
19. *Ibid.*, p. 21.
20. *As I Remember*, p. 111.
21. Derick Thomson, "A Man Reared in Lewis" in *As I Remember*, p.124: p. 133.
22. Private correspondence with Derick Thomson, 25 August 1987.
23. *Ibid.*
24. *Towards the Human*, p. 42; "Writing in Gaelic," *Lines Review*, 33 (July, 1970), pp. 3-9 (3).
25. Finlay J. Macdonald, *Crowdie and Cream: Memoirs of a Hebridean Childhood* (London: Futura, 1983), pp. 64-5.
26. *The Last Summer* (London: Gollancz, 1969), p. 9.
27. *The Law and The Grace* (London: Eyre & Spottiswoode, 1965), p. 16; p. 34.
28. "Writers and Education," *Scottish Education Journal* (31 October 1975), 1010-1011 (p. 1010).
29. *Ibid.*
30. "My Relationship With Poetry," *Chapman*, 16, 4:4 (Summer 1976) 12-18 (p. 13).
31. "Writers and Education," p. 1010.
32. See, for example, *Towards the Human*, p. 24.
33. *The Last Summer*, p. 78.
34. For a fuller treatment of Lacan's relevance to Crichton Smith's work, see "Iain Crichton Smith: A Poetry of Opposition," my PhD Thesis. University of Dundee, 1989.
35. *My Last Duchess* (London: Gollancz, 1971), p. 158.
36. Radio Talk, "Scottish Life and Letters," BBC Scottish Home Service, October 13 1963.
37. "My Relationship With Poetry," p. 18.
38. *Towards the Human*, p. 51.
39. *Ibid.*, p. 26.

II
Away

CHAPTER TWO

The Diamond-Browed One

Iain Crichton Smith's poetry has frequently been classed as a poetry of opposition, a poetry of "conflict" and "paradoxes and tensions."[1] The description is reinforced by the poet's own terms, a "war between two opposites" and "dichotomy" and is foregrounded by the titles of many of the volumes themselves: *Thistles and Roses, The Law and the Grace, Bibles and Advertisements.*[2] Discussion of these volumes tends to see them in a way which roots them in the Scottish tradition exemplified by MacDiarmid's jubilant boast, "I'll ha'e nae hauf-way hoose, but aye be whaur / Extremes meet."[3] At the beginning of this century, Gregory Smith's term, "Caledonian Antisyzygy," described oppositions he claimed were inherent in Scottish culture.[4] Over sixty years later, Alan Bold's label is "internal division."[5] Ronnie Turnbull and Craig Beveridge take issue with this tendency to define Scottish culture in a negative way "as something freakish and pathological" and suggest it stems from an anti-Scottish prejudice. They cite the following quotation from a 1976 article about R. D. Laing in support of their claim:

> Clearly Dr Laing is himself somewhat divided, as are so many Scotsmen. Highlands and Lowlands, cold rationalists and Calvinistic fanatics, Glasgow and Edinburgh, teetotallers and and dram-drinkers. Perhaps *The Divided Self* should be seen in a tradition that includes such other works by Scots such as Stevenson's *Dr Jekyll and Mr Hyde*, and Hogg's *Confessions of a Justified Sinner.*[6]

The divided Scot may seem a tired old label but perhaps few Scottish writers could deny its truth: missing from the list above is the head and the heart—the conflict and division created by a mother tongue and an

English education which engages most Scottish writers at some stage in their careers. Many would insist that it is only once the head and the heart are harmonised that they can write well. Billy Kay describes the moment when, as a fifteen-year-old, he read Grassic Gibbon's *Sunset Song*, and discovered, recognised, his own culture: head and heart, the language and culture of his own home and his ideas of "literature," came together.[7] But for Crichton Smith, division has proved fruitful. His early work shows a movement away from his background, positing against that perceived negative a poetry which achieves an other-worldly resolution. Against the Gaelic matriarch, the black-hatted Calvinist, the single-minded Puritan, he sets images of grace. Defined by its opposite, grace is freedom, youth, beauty, art and complexity. What is important, however, is not the binaries he creates, but his exploration of them. Setting up a self separate from his background, he explores the oppositions of restriction and freedom, a self defined by the place and time in which he was born, and a self created in the poetry. But almost as soon as these neat, geometric oppositions are constructed, they begin to collapse. Already there are images of intrusion, where the historical world breaks in on his other-world of poetry; and in the long sequence "Deer On The High Hills," the discovery is made that these binaries themselves need to be deconstructed.

The first volume, *The Long River*, published in 1955, is a poetic manifesto from a young poet dedicating himself to his craft. With hindsight, Crichton Smith identifies the weakness of this first volume: "it . . . is composed of lyrics, not very closely anchored to a recognisable reality, aching for meaning and 'beauty'."[8] During the time these poems were written, Crichton Smith was living in Dumbarton and Helensburgh. Behind him were his experiences of National Service, and he had begun his career as a teacher. Yet the places, the experiences, do not find a presence in a first volume peopled by Auden, MacDiarmid, Shelley, Burns, Sappho, Blake and Clare. The language of *The Long River* is a world of textuality, inhabited by individuals who are constructs of their texts. This other-world of literature denies that poetry is situated *in* the world, a world where men and women talk, eat *and* write poems.

The most important figure in that world is W. H. Auden, who represents the antithesis of Calvinist Lewis. Against the Free Church Crichton Smith sets a free spirit:

I was a great admirer of Auden in those days when I was young. I suppose I thought of him as a kind of free spirit in a sense as against the Bible side of it.[9]

The admiration is apparent in the first volume. "The Dedicated

Spirits" offers an Auden-like *paysage moralisé* of ice and sterility. Images of night, dormancy and paralysis are cut by images of light, life and movement. Yet around him the poet sees only confirmation of his own isolation: "About us the horizon bends / its orphan images."[10] This landscape is devoid of its people, its community. Lewis is a treeless, lochan-strewn landscape, composed of gneiss, among the oldest rock in the British Isles. During the Ice Ages, huge glaciers gouged out the lochs and scraped away the good soil. A solitary tree may defy the landscape but to the poet it reflects only his desperate solitude. The images here create an ice-age of the imagination, of tradition. The poet is trapped, "Turning on the icy wheel / of image without substance."[11] Like the Romantic poets, Crichton Smith is caught in a circular pattern in which his movement towards illumination brings him back to the reality he seeks to escape. He is trapped, too, by the language of the English poets he has read, a mixture of Modernism and Romanticism. The images of footsteps, of horizon and orphan, of the mapless navigator, suggest not only the lack of anchor, of rootedness, but also the overpowering influence of Auden.

"Meditation Addressed to Hugh MacDiarmid" addresses a fellow poet, a companion in this other world. If Auden represented an alien, English tradition, perhaps in MacDiarmid the poet could find a father-figure? Certainly there are surface similarities: both were bookish, solitary figures, and shared a boyhood of poor health. Both rebelled against a tradition they saw as sterile. MacDiarmid was attracted to the large themes that were to attract Crichton Smith. Yet surface similarities cannot conceal basic differences. Crichton Smith's choice of language was between his native Gaelic and the English of his education. Although MacDiarmid saw Scotland's tradition as rooted in Gaelic, Scots was his own tongue and that is the language he tried to enrich. There is a public quality and a robustness to MacDiarmid which is alien to Crichton Smith. Comparison of a few lines from "Meditation Addressed to Hugh MacDiarmid" and MacDiarmid's "To Circumjack Cencrastus," illustrates the point neatly:

> The question is: was ever voice heard calling
> its absolute notes through the Newtonian woods
> or was it a child we constantly heard bawling
> and crawling into small decrepitudes?[12]

MacDiarmid poses his question directly, familiarly:

> O Knowledge, wha can tell
> That o' ye ilka bit is
> No' juist a dodge to hide faur mair?[13]

MacDiarmid uses traditional personification whereas Crichton Smith uses the diminished abstraction of "small decrepitudes." MacDiarmid's lines illuminate Crichton Smith's more delicate probing: MacDiarmid confronts the question squarely, Crichton Smith is nervous of the answer.

Given these essential differences it is small wonder that Crichton Smith's MacDiarmid is a strange, silent interlocutor. The poet plunges into images of reawakening and rebirth. "Our love" is the persistent spirit, the long river, the poet's commitment:

> Let our love speak before the horseman rides
> into nocturnal chambers heavy with dew.
> Let the locks break and the original tides
> inhabit the dead granite and construe
> spellings and conjugations from our sides
> and all the verbs of being rise renewed
> above voluminous waters where all brides
> unfold their breasts and wake to find us true.[14]

A self-generated escape ends in an orgy of textuality: "construe," "spellings and conjugations," "verbs of being," and "voluminous" testify to the other-worldliness of his poems.

In the other-world he calls the roll: Catullus, Shelley, Burns, Sappho, Blake and Clare. Yet these are solitary figures, offering him a role-model of superior isolation:

> the diamond-browed one stands
> horizons and seas beyond
> the habitable land[15]

The poet of *The Long River* is "the diamond-browed one" who finds identity only in isolation and transcendence.

Yet even in this first volume there is a tentative movement to establish his poetry *in* the world. The title, "On Helensburgh Sea Front," suggests a poet standing in a real place but the wish is to "abolish from my verse" the "I" and "my" and "mine," to deny time and place and transcend everyday reality. The qualification in "even that man with rivered cheeks" and

> even that woman heavy-eyed
> nursing the twilight to her bone
> and stopping the holes in her dumb side
> with music from the gramophone[16]

separates the poet from the man and woman here. Identity is beginning to be formed by a process of opposition. The practical man is representative not just of physical labourer but of the poet's culture: in Lewis, Crichton Smith has noted, "the most important thing was to be practical and I wasn't that."[17] The woman offers another opposition; the woman content with popular art "stopping the holes in her dumb side" is set apart from the poet in "Prometheus" who bares his side:

> O great red eagle plunge
> from the top of the snowed rock,
> sharpen your terrible beak
> on mercy's stone and drive
> in blood in a raging storm
> to waken my heart alive[18]

and from the writer who has said that writing poetry "is a frightening thing, as if one's personality is being opened out with a knife. So poetry can be both a terror and an adventure."[19] The woman is passive receiver and "dumb": she is constructed in and by popular culture. The poet needs to speak for himself, to create and discover himself. The image for this task is borrowed from the Gaelic poet, William Ross: "a blind man hunting a key / on a night of terror and storm."[20]

If Billy Kay describes his discovery of *Sunset Song* as the discovery of self, of harmony, of a basis from which to write, Crichton Smith does not discover self but rather attempts to create self: a self in opposition to the culture in which he was raised. In "Poem of Lewis," his island is the time and place which he sets apart from his poetry:

> Here they have no time for the fine graces
> of poetry, unless it freely grows
> in deep compulsion, like water in the well,
> woven into the texture of the soil
> in a strong pattern.

The poem ends on an apocalyptic moment of destruction, typical of the early work, "and the early daffodil, purer than a soul, / is gathered into the terrible mouth of the gale."[21]

"It Was A Country" hints that the creation of a self, an "I" on a blank page, is a delusion. Lewis is the blank page and the poem explores the sense of importance of the boy who will imprint on this clean, fresh landscape his own history, innocently: "There was nothing to be done / but let your shadow in the water lie."[22] The ambiguity in "lie" prefigures the truth that comes with an image of war, caught just off the frame. "A strange plane" is the metaphor for the feeling of change and danger experienced, which comes

> bearing a future which the heart must trace
> in beams of blood across the tranquil sky
> now soft as grace.[23]

The early poetry is poetry of the head, of his English reading and English education. The change of imagery from "shadow in the water" to "beams of blood across the tranquil sky" suggests a change from the lie to the truth, the head to the heart, and reveals a painful, dangerous journey. The poem predicts the development towards a self anchored in time and place, and towards the discovery:

> One cannot run away, he thought to himself as he walked towards the house. Or if one runs away one cannot be happy anywhere any more. If one left in the first place one could never go back. Or if one came back one also brought a virus, an infection of time and place. One always brings back a judgment to one's home.[24]

The metaphor of the virus is grounded in the reality of the fisher girls who left Lewis and returned with the infection of TB which threatened to destroy a community. The poet's fate is to be anchored in time and place, a Lewisman, but also the stranger. Crichton Smith's work explores such divisions and complexities. And if this places him firmly within a tradition, it is hard to see that it is to define his work in a negative way. A cultural tradition which includes such works as *Dr Jekyll and Mr Hyde* and *Confessions of a Justified Sinner* is a rich one indeed. And if the oppositions implied by the titles of the early volumes are neatly geometric, if they come from the head rather than the heart, very soon they begin to collapse.

Crichton Smith's first volume reveals a poet enchanted with language, rebelling against the austerity of his background. There is a richness of metaphor, of unexpected images, and a sensuous, free play. Yet the desire to find a base for his art, to root it in reality, demands he admit into his work its opposite. The embodiment of that opposite is the Gaelic matriarch, the "old woman" inscribed again and again as other. In many ways, the delineation of the old woman is a cleansing: identifying her, he cleanses himself of his background, the time and place in which he was born.

The volumes which follow, *The White Noon, Thistles and Roses, The Law and The Grace*, show the poet identifying more closely the sensed opposition. The "old woman" becomes the symbol of everything that opposes his art because she is stamped with the mark of Calvinism and death, the greatest tests for his poetry. Crichton Smith's preoccupation with old women is perhaps connected with the fact that he was raised by a widowed mother, in a society where the old predominated and the young men of the island had gone off to war. "Growing up among an ageing population . . . I seem to know more about the old than I do about the young."[25] Women in general are perhaps seen by him as more entrenched in their society. Men from the island frequently enjoyed a wider experience. Many were sailors, travelling world-wide.

The war forced many men to leave the island. The conflict implied in the memoir "Between Sea and Moor" is between the sea, the larger opportunities opening up for the young boy, and the moor, his closed Gaelic culture. It might be argued that the young Lewis fisher girls also left to follow the herring fleets and gut the fish, but the comparisons in the poem "For My Mother" between the seventeen-year-old university student and the seventeen-year-old fisher girl are between "more" and "less," between sipping "good learning" and "gutting herring." Such inequalities bring guilt:

> Angrily I watch you from my guilt
> and sometimes think: The herring in my hand,
> bloody and gutted, would be far more solid
> than this more slippery verse.[26]

Interviewed in 1972, Crichton Smith agreed with Lorn Macintyre's assessment of that guilt:

> You believe that your intelligence, your talents, and your university education alienated you, not only from your mother, but from Lewis, its people and its history. In a sense you are apologising for the "fine graces" of your poetry, and also teaching yourself a lesson in humility.[27]

There is no doubt that for the young Gael education was synonymous with alienation. Yet Macintyre's comment assumes responsibility. In fact, choices were not made by, but made for, both fisher girl and poet. Both were claimed by their societies: she became a fisher girl as did her peers; he was processed through the education system. Though his mother left to follow the herring she stayed within a community of fisher girls. To be a fisher girl was to be part of a group, to have a shared identity. It was the practice for a minister from the island to accompany a group of fisher girls who left to follow the herring fleet and administer to their spiritual needs. They took Calvinism with them.[28] A poet on Lewis had no peers: "I felt myself as alienated from my own friends for I had the feeling that I was predestined to be a writer—a poet certainly."[29] That sense of alienation was compounded by his education, by the influence of the canon of English poetry.

The Gaelic Matriarch, the old woman of Crichton Smith's poetry, is a complex of images. She represents the power of the Calvinist background, the suppression of individuality, of joy, of art. She is rooted in the real historical world—a world whose trump card is death. Yet she is also admired for her stubbornness, her dedication, and for her power. For a poet who constantly examines and dismantles the very bases of his art, her rigid identity itself is both repulsive and attractive. Crichton Smith's poems about old women explore such complexities. "They have been condemned in some way to a narrower life than we have," he has said, and illuminates clearly that these poems neither seek to condemn nor to praise but rather to set down, to record, without false sympathy, lives that are circumscribed, narrowed, and yet endured.[30]

"Old Woman" makes use of a three-line stanza with one unrhymed, and two rhymed or slant rhymed lines which foreground the unrhymed "back," "mouth," "eyes," and "hands." Yet this is no encomium. The physical features are described not for beauty but for purpose. A back bears the heavy creel, hands rock a sinful cradle, eyes are the senses through which a hard world intrudes itself:

> Your cold eyes
> watched your drunken husband come
> unsteadily from Sodom home.[31]

The woman's yellow hair, purposelessly beautiful in a world where beauty is irrelevant, when it cannot work or mend, is concealed till it fades:

> Your yellow hair
> burned slowly in a scarf of grey
> wildly falling like the mountain spray.[32]

Beside this world the poet sets his images of grace and beauty, allowing now rhyme on all three lines:

> while the free daffodils
> wave in the valleys and on the hills
> the deer look down with their instinctive skills.[33]

These images are also images of indifference and detachment: a beauty and a grace surviving because they cannot share the woman's experience of the world, an experience which has shaped her. They belong to a different world, a world set above or beside her world. That "while" establishes their co-existence and their separation. Her beauty is concealed and negated while theirs flourishes. The poet brings his image of the daffodil into the poem like a gift to the woman, aware always that it is irrelevant and will be dismissed or even destroyed: "you steadily stamped the rising daffodil."[34] The separation of beauty, the "free daffodil" and "the deer" from this Calvinist landscape reveals clearly how much poetry is other-worldly. Crichton Smith's education, his reading, have shaped a world from the text of English poetry, not the Calvinist bible. His description of the landscape of the north-east Scots poet George Bruce also suggests the reasons why this poem posits beauty and harshness side by side to describe only a gulf:

It is, as he himself says, a "land without myth," and he is never tempted to import into it alien opulences of language. It is a land of hard light. . . . It is a land where towns seem slightly irrelevant against ageless rocks and sea: it is an almost anti-poetic land that requires a terse language, abrupt, physical. It is an astringent land.[35]

Even today, to see the thin, straggling village of Bayble huddled low on a grey horizon, strung between sea and moor, is to appreciate the appropriateness of such a comment to Lewis, and to understand the source of the oppositions in Crichton Smith's work.

This, then, is his land, and his people. An "anti-poetic" land and a people symbolised by the Gaelic matriarch: hostile and threatening. Such a culture creates such a people. "Schoolteacher," "The Widow" and "Statement By A Responsible Spinster," offer careful, steady portraits. Carefully, they label the spectre, the face of Calvinism: steadily they account for such lives. The first two lines of "Schoolteacher," "She was always earlier than the bell at nine. / She trod the same stone street for forty years," form the epitaph for an unremarked, unremarkable life.[36] The end-stopped lines insist that there is indeed little further to be said and suggest reluctance, reticence and tact; reluctance to engage with the spectre, perhaps, and the recognition of a sense of intrusion. They are the physical embodiment of a structured, determined, narrowed life. Yet within that structure, the schoolteacher survives, she endures. The enjambment of the remaining lines open up the poem and invest the blurred imagery of her life with activity and purpose and at the same time create a sense of confusion which is halted by a sudden moment of questioning: "What was the message she had tried to tell / for forty years?"[37] Identity is imprisoned by that label, "schoolteacher." The poet juxtaposes images to bring about the poem's conclusion and reveal the sterility of that identity. Her "barren gown" is set against the red apple hissing. Apple and serpent become one, symbol of temptation and experience, to be locked away: "The apple lay / placed in her loved desk, soon to decay."[38] Crichton Smith recognises that his old women are locked into an identity forged by internalised outside forces.

"Old Highland Woman Reading Newspaper" reveals the process of attraction and repulsion:

> bent over print and old remorseless hands
> grasping these deaths, the tombstones all in white
> her eyes traverse with gritty appetite
> in the slow justice of her mouth's small sounds.[39]

The survivor gloats over these deaths, but the poet's image of her is

C

of a body already dead, the tombstone in place. Words which suggest physical decay, frailty, ambiguously suggest the qualities of stubbornness and dutifulness to which the poet appears reluctantly attracted. "Gritty" suggests eye strain, yet also the idea of pluck. "Grasping" suggests an inability to exert fine muscle control, a greed, a "gritty appetite," yet also suggests her fearlessness and her acceptance of the fact of death. "Bent over" suggests the physical posture of old age, yet also the intense concentration directed towards these obituaries. "Old remorseless hands" are hands which display the inevitable decay, the approach of death, yet exhibit no fear.

"The Witches" offers a society of old women and ends "pity them, pity them. Dare / to ring them with your love."[40] Is that dare directed at the reader or the poet himself? The multiple meanings of "ring" open out in a spiral. The women can be ringed like birds, suggesting identification, ownership—and therefore the sense of claiming. Ring also suggests the marriage ring, betrothal and love. Yet more importantly it foregrounds the circle: the act of exclusion and separation. The titles of these poems are always labels: "Old Woman," "Schoolteacher," "Old Highland Woman Reading Newspaper" suggest the titles of paintings and effectively label the spectre. These titles label otherness, and all that Crichton Smith finds negative. He draws a circle round separate experiences, an action which is ambiguous. It offers him a positive identity in opposition to theirs, unfettered by the constraints of physical life—where poetry, art, can draw such a circle and exist outside it. Unacknowledged as yet is the fact that the drawing of a boundary imprisons the poet, too, in exclusion.

"Grace" is what the poet sets against the old woman, thistle, law and bible. Grace belongs, but temporarily, to the young girls of Iain Crichton Smith's poetry. In them he celebrates beauty, a natural ease, a sense of being at home in the world. Yet their grace is vulnerable: young girls are shaped and moulded by their society of Calvinist Lewis, and sometimes by the education system. "Schoolgirl on Speech Day" celebrates a youthful freedom but sees inevitably boundaries, definition and containment. Against the youth of the girl is set the weighty authority of the "bald official men." The metaphor of the circle celebrates her freedom from it, but holds it ever present: "no ring of shadow has engaged her pride / or wolfed her, fallen, in the circling night," and in contrast to the "set mouth" of his old woman, this mouth smiles, it alters shape, and suggests a quality of surplus: "A smile plays round / her unstained lips, as if a joke would spill."[41] "Unstained" is both physical and moral—it hints, too, at a freedom from the ideology inscribed in language, an innocence. The poet raised in a Gaelic culture is inscribed in that culture through the language he is offered. Rejecting it, attempting to find a new language with which to express himself, he inscribes himself. The possibility of the spilling joke offers the possibility of surplus, the joke as imaginative use of language and more simply, the idea of profane laughter. Yet with "And then I turn again" the poet moves from a celebration of grace to the idea of enclosure, the circle again: "and think how thirty years can fence a man / by what he loses and by what he wins."[42] "Thirty years" have built fences, forged a life, and the girl will be subject to a similar fate. The poet, standing outside the man and viewing both "she" and "he," transcends them both.

Grace is freedom from the circle that constrains, circumscribes. The "bald official men" are the officials of the education system who have the power to encircle, to subject. Crichton Smith's own experience of the education system would make him sensitive to such power. His experience as a teacher informs those poems which deal with the young in education. Indeed, one of the reasons which lay behind his decision to retire from teaching in 1977 was a distaste for the power his position carried:

> I wouldn't like to exert . . . any form of power over anyone else . . . and the thing is that if you are a teacher then you are exerting power over people. It can be intellectual power and latterly I didn't feel that I'd the right almost to exert this kind of power.[43]

Education separated him from his background. Education offered him a "world beyond this world." Education offered liberation—and loss. These contradictions and complexities are explored in "Young Highland Girl Studying Poetry" which offers an image of the power which both makes and mars: "Poetry drives its lines into her forehead / like an angled plough across a bare field."[44] Poetry, education, is like an "angled plough" which has the power to uproot this young, vulnerable girl. Yet her culture is seen as a strong one. "The foreign rose abated at their mouth" shows the rose, the symbol of the antithesis to an austere Calvinist ethic in *Thistles and Roses*, subdued, negated, by something equally strong. For these people have their own natural culture, beliefs, superstition, music. They have grown out of the land. And yet these strengths imprison within the circle. The poem is a complex one: it sees how a culture can limit and contain, and yet it expresses a sense of loss, a tribute to the kind of culture that has produced such a girl, and from which he is for ever alienated—and from which he, as teacher, may alienate her, too. The positive and negative aspects of community combine here. "For most must walk though some by natural flying / learn from the bitter winds a kind of praise" suggests the "chilly air of pure individuality."[45] It places the poet in an austere and aristocratic position characteristic of the early work.

35

Crichton Smith sees the classroom as a place of opposition and conflict. The Apollonian confronts the Dionysian. His comments made at the time of the teachers' strike in 1985 suggested sympathy with Apollo:

> I know that many other occupations are stressful but teachers often have to deal with the irrational and their lives can be made hellish unless they can control a class.[46]

Yet Apollo is austere and distant. Remembering teachers from his past "who were so frightening that it was difficult to learn from them," and who were "tall formidable presences usually dispensing punishment . . . distant presences administering what was supposed to be a constant ethos," he can also sympathise with the Dionysian.[47] In "Schoolteacher" he explores the division between ruler and ruled. This schoolteacher rules her class in her "distant gown" like a latter-day Roman, educating, civilising, colonising. The schoolchildren are taught the politics of power; they learn about submission and revolt and "how the empires fade / is wild barbarians at 4 o'clock." His sympathy is with the barbarians here:

> A swirl of gown along a marble hall
> is too inhuman for their festival,
> the snigger of their rigorous black gods.[48]

Placed in "Schoolroom Incident" on the side of Apollo, the poet is crushed by guilt. His dreams are peopled by Nazis in boots; teacher and pupil are both victims:

> The moon remembers desolate waste fires.
> The ashen storm
> is (I submit) both his and hers and mine.[49]

Cast in the role of educator he is cast in a position of power, a position which encircles, defines, and corrupts, both self and others.

In "Rythm" (*sic*) the schoolboy's grace is exemplified by his language which breaks all the rules:

> The ball's at your feet and there it goes, just crack.
> Old Jerry dives—the wrong way. And they're jearing
> and I run to the centre and old Bash
> jumps up and down, and I feel great, and wearing
> my gold and purpel strip, fresh from the wash.[50]

The chain of repetitive "ands" suddenly springs into life with "and wearing" where head and heart harmonise, and the boy finds unity of mind and body, a grace in the world.

Significantly, the child who finds grace is male. Women are always the vulnerable ones. The woman is seen as more firmly entrenched in her background and therefore any attack on that figure will offer him maximum opposition, a greater degree of conflict. Crichton Smith's best known novel, *Consider the Lilies*, takes as its heroine just such a woman, a woman possessed of the meagreness and narrowness of the Calvinist state of mind, but in tracing her development in the novel, Crichton Smith traces the development of an individual who is locked away within the cage of an ideology to one who is more open to the world. Two quotations will illustrate this development:

> Her mother had put a stop to all that—the dances, the ceilidhs. No one could tell how she had become possessed by the fear of hell in her latter days.[51]

> "You're doing very well," said Donald Macleod, coming in smiling. But she knew that she wasn't and that she couldn't tell a proper story. All the time she had got more and more muddled and she didn't even know how the story was to end.[52]

Springing the cage of ideology is not easy, and Mrs Scott's difficulty over her story-telling to the children of the atheist Macleod posits her outside the circle which constrains but which yet offers a fixed identity. Not knowing how the story is to end posits an open, undefined Mrs Scott, too.

A poetry of opposition explores the cages which constrain, and yet which offer a sense of identity, and sets against that defined, confined position an identity outside the circle, open to possibility and neither defined nor confined but in the process of being written. "Grace" is never found within the circle: in "A Note on Puritans," the poet can admire the search for truth, the stubbornness of the faith, but he rejects a single-mindedness which has led to brutishness:

> I accuse
> these men of singleness and loss of grace
> who stared so deeply into the fire's hues
> that all was fire to them.[53]

If the image of the daffodil and the deer represents grace, the opposition to Calvinist Lewis, in a poetry of clean geometry, the image of the vase symbolises the harmony of warring elements in the poetry. "Studies in Power" shows the poet momentarily doubting the "cardboard coins" of his poems as he sits at a business meeting, yet achieving that state of grace:

> Till suddenly there I saw a vase in bloom
> gathering light about it clearly clearly
> in adult daylight not by a moon obscurely,

and its harder language filled the small room
with its bare constant self, its paradigm
of straining forces harmonised sincerely.[54]

In "Three Sonnets," however, that stage of grace is more precarious, more temporary. This is acknowledged as a created harmony, a "parenthetic calm":

as if you were
a brimming vase struck from the various pack
of cloud and leaf, dependent not on luck
but necessary form, correct and rare. . . .

This momentary easing of a tension
crowns you a queen, between the dark and light.[55]

Grace is achieved by bracketing off the flux of the world around him. But placing in brackets the historical world, achieving a state of grace in the other-world of his poetry, effectively isolates the poet from the real world and the "tumultuous chaos."[56] Such grace is questioned.

Crichton Smith's early poetry, then, can usefully be described as a poetry of opposition and coming from a strong Scottish tradition. But it is important to stress that these created oppositions are constantly tested, and their boundaries re-drawn. The neat, geometric poetry created by the head is constantly undermined—the omissions, the falsities of his system which creates a state of grace are worked out and worked through on the imaginative level. There are two poems which offer important landmarks in the poet's early work because they reveal clearly an honest failure to achieve a state of grace. I have suggested that the old woman is the greatest test for his poetry because she is stamped with the mark of Calvinism and death. "Old Woman" and "Sunday Morning Walk" encounter specifically the most basic fact of the historical world—death.

The first line of "Old Woman" offers not just description, but condition: "and she, being old, fed from a mashed plate." "Being old" is not merely descriptive as "mashed" is. It is her ongoing condition, her label, her sin—and most importantly, her cage. Age, infirmity, highlight body. The poet shows impatience with the religion of the old couple as the husband prays

to God who is all-forgiving to send down
some angel somewhere who might land perhaps
in his foreign wings among the gradual crops.[57]

The deliberate vagueness of "some," "somewhere," "might" and "perhaps" and most damning of all, "foreign," makes clear that the husband's prayers will go unanswered: such grace is foreign to such a place, such a time, such a condition. The poet's response is one of anger and sympathy and an inability either to accept or to transcend this scene. Where once the poet may have achieved a state of grace removed from the historical world, this poem switches to a deliberately borrowed, heightened, Keatsian tone invoking the Nightingale Ode and another world of art:

> and wished to be away, yes, to be far away
> with athletes, heroes, Greeks or Roman men
> who pushed their bitter spears into a vein
> and would not spend an hour with such decay.[58]

Here is not a slow dehumanising decline into infirmity but the glorious death of legend. If the old woman's husband seeks shelter under the umbrella of his island's religion, he makes the poet aware that he too seeks a similar false resolution. The invoking of Classical literature, of Romantic poetry, is an escape. Yet the word "wish" leaves the poet "imprisoned," transcendence denied.

"Sunday Morning Walk" also contrasts Classical myth with a physical reality. It offers a poet who flees the sun on the streets and the Sunday bells for the tranquillity of the woods. On the way, he passes a castle which in its seeming permanence, reminds him that he is a "pack of wandering flesh" like the sheep he is to encounter. "Holiday" is what he seeks in opposition to this holy day. Yet this is denied him. While he is enjoying his walk, enjoying the sensuousness of his well-being, his mind is turning on Classical mythology. With "And occupied thus, I came where a dead sheep lay" there is a *peripeteia*. His imaginative freedom is dashed by the reality before him. The description of the dead sheep, and of the flies buzzing around it, is detailed for the next six verses. The repetition of "how quickly" and "how" which begins at the end of the sixth verse and continues throughout the seventh suggests language stuck in a groove, stuttering. Death threatens to have the last word here:

> How quickly, how quickly
> the wool was peeled from the back. How still was the flesh.
> How the visiting flies would not knock at the door of the sockets.
> How the hole in the side gaped red, a well-sized gash.
> How the clear young lambs grazed in the shade of the thickets.[59]

The image of the visiting flies who would not knock seems to be tied up with the Gaelic background, and the sense of threat experienced by the lack of privacy and individuality. The image of the hole is characteristic of the early poetry. At a deep level, the image suggests a death of the poetic response. The poet is stopped in his tracks by this scene of death, by the antithesis to his imaginary world of sensuality and immortal Gods:

> The jaw, well-shaved, lay slackly
> there on the warm quiet grass. The household air
> was busy with buzzing like fever.[60]

The verse shimmers in and out of focus here with that "jaw, well-shaved." Sometimes we see a description of the sheep and sometimes we see a description of the poet himself, a human death, a domestic scene. In this moment of shock, the distance between poet and sheep disappears.

With the line, "And the sun blazed hot on my shoulder. Here was no shade" there is the recognition that though the poet has sought escape, has sought "holiday" from the fire of the sun on the streets, he has not found it. He has turned his back on the tight-locked streets and those men he sees imprisoned within the circle of their religion. Yet inside that circle they have a way of coping with death. The poet's mythology distracts him but cannot shield him from the reality he encounters. Involved in his literary musings, he is suddenly confronted by a death's head.

Identity for the early poet is an identity in a "world beyond this world," and his illumination is achieved by bracketing off the historical world. Yet that movement towards illumination and grace is sometimes halted, particularly in poems where the opposition against which he tests his poetry is death. What is important about the poetry of opposition is the way in which these oppositions are explored. I have shown how resolution comes to be seen as created by the poet, to be temporary, or parenthetic. I have shown how images of death represent a reality that intrudes, that disturbs the perfection of a created grace. The image of intrusion is important. Crichton Smith's first volume offered a poet of brilliant metaphor and dazzling language: he becomes a poet of major status when that created grace is undermined and disturbed not by placing it against its opposite, but by allowing it to be explored on the imaginative level, allowing the poet to become discoverer of his own meanings, reader of his own work.

In 1972, Crichton Smith published "Deer on the High Hills," a long poem which offers a completely new perspective and scrutinises the leap which takes him into the "world beyond this world." Crichton Smith's comments about how the poem came to be written are relevant here because they insist on a process of discovery. If in the early poetry of opposition the self-contained binaries shift and collapse, continually decentring the poet's position, "Deer on the High Hills" prompts the discovery that his moments of illumination and grace offer too simple a solution: the sequence offers a poet poised midway between a poetry of grace and a poetry which leads to silence.

Crichton Smith has spoken on many occasions of the roots of the poem. Driving home from Glasgow one evening he noticed deer at the side of the road. He had also been reading Dante, which may account for the three-line structure of the poem. The poem was written quickly and he confesses that he finds it a strange poem, one that he cannot account for or fully understand, though he recognises its importance. What is important, perhaps, to Crichton Smith, is that the poem seems to be unauthorised, to come from that part of the creative impulse which he has termed the "imagination." Commending the "hallucinatory quality" of MacDiarmid's "The Watergaw" in 1972, Crichton Smith insisted

> Whatever the imagination is, there is no doubt that it is what we require in poetry at the highest level. How it operates is incomprehensible. What it creates is, strictly speaking, incapable of being managed by the mind.[61]

Crichton Smith's satisfaction with the poem seems to be this quality of imagination which allows the poet to become reader of his own work. In "Deer On The High Hills," the deer, the early symbol of grace, is questioned and analysed. The poet contemplates the deer not just as symbol but as part of the animal world, as an observable fact in the historical world. Yet symbol or animal, language contaminates both and the distinction cannot be maintained. The language shifts and bends as the poet explores on the imaginative level the bases of his own poetry.

Seven years later, Crichton Smith was to publish a translation of Duncan Ban Macintyre's "Ben Dòrain." His introduction to that translation perhaps offers to illuminate the meaning of the deer in "Deer On The High Hills." Pondering what he sees as a growing interest in animals in contemporary poetry, Crichton Smith observed, "I have a feeling that it arises from the failure of man as seen after the concentration camps." He goes on to deny any charge of escapism:

> It arises from wanting to know what the world of the animal is really like. Is it like our own? Is an animal more an animal than a human being is a human being? Hughes talks of the Pike being "pike in all parts." No Hamlets in the animal world, no ruined liberals.[62]

The qualities he finds to commend in the animal world are defined negatively: no Hamlets, no ruined liberals. Interestingly, the qualities he finds to commend in Duncan Ban Macintyre are similarly defined negatively:

> This is a great poem by a sane balanced man who looked out on his world and saw that it was good in spite of the blood. In fact it was his job to hunt. He was not a neurotic. It was not his job to seek relationships. He would never have dreamed of using the deer as

symbols for anything. . . . Nor would he use "Ben Dòrain" as a field for the rotting liberal imagination, which confuses animals with men so that the latter lose their identity.[63]

Perhaps it was because of Macintyre's achievement that Crichton Smith's meditation ponders the symbol and moves towards an exploration of language itself.

The first section assumes the power of epigraph as the poet is confronted by the gaze of the deer which is also the gaze of the real world—and therefore of the death's head: "A deer looks through you to the other side, / and what it is and sees is an inhuman pride."[64] This is an astringent, bracing moment. Comments made by Crichton Smith about MacDiarmid's "On A Raised Beach" seem to me to illuminate why this couplet generates excitement. Crichton Smith commended those moments in MacDiarmid's poem when

> the poet sees the stones naked in front of him and yet at the same time as shining with the distance that is really between them and him. At those moments the poet is not being animistic, he is making no assumptions. The stones truly are distant, inhuman, and therefore they become a true image for the inhumanity that he feels he needs . . . this is the true inhuman object staring back at that which wishes to be the same.[65]

The poet who "sees," creates the deer, and makes them the property of his consciousness, not something in the outside world "out there." Seeing is a creative act. The act of creation is always historical: the seer is constituted by time and place. Crichton Smith's early poems, rejecting time and place, attempt to draw boundaries between a personal history and to write from the point of view of an "I" who is "horizons and seas beyond / the habitable land"—an "I" who is inhuman.[66] For the poet to see and yet see the deer "shining with the distance that is really between them and him" posits a double act. It produces a language which draws attention to its artificiality yet which strangely can see those deer "naked." The "staring back" suggests a poet who can meet the gaze without flinching—the gaze that troubles, like the blind beggar, the "old woman," or the death's head of his "Sunday Morning Walk."

Drawing attention to its artificiality, the poem shifts from the referential towards a series of similes:

> Yesterday three deer stood at the roadside.
> It was icy January and there they were
> like debutantes on a smooth ballroom floor.[67]

The first two lines form flat observation: a statement of numbers, place, time, like a composition of a scene for analysis. "And there they were"

42

positioned at the line-end enacts a sense of being locked out by this description. The poet seems to clamber out painfully with similes instead of his more usual powerful metaphor. The weaker simile appears more artful, it draws attention to itself. The position of "like" at the beginning of the last line above and after the caesura in the second stanza in "like Louis the Sixteenth" draws attention to the poet's cognitive approach, to the artificiality of it. The alliteration in "deer" and "debutante" is important because it highlights the audacity of the conceit, the incongruity of linking together a wild animal and a stereotype of class, breeding, artificiality. In many ways the deer, too, offer a stereotyped image: Landseer's "Monarch of the Glen" meets the English debutante. Yet such juxtaposition, such audacious incongruity, offers new illumination and the comparison captures something more revealing than the bare statement of the opening two lines of section II. The imagination of the poet creates the deer. "There they were" holds them at a distance, intractable, invisible to us. It is only the poet's imagination, his perception, which allows the reader to see them. Yet when the poet "sees" he contaminates. In "Deer On The High Hills" the conflict is between the desire to resist the symbol, and the desire to "see." Seeing is a creative act, and in that act, the poet discovers a kind of truth. I have already shown how Crichton Smith has insisted that poetry of the highest order is worked out on the imaginative level, a level that escapes the mind. Kant also drew a veil round the creative act, separating as Crichton Smith does the rational from the creative, insisting on the mystery of creativity.[68] Crichton Smith's insistence on how this poem came to be written claims just such mystery. He has also drawn tight boundaries between reason and imagination. "Deer On The High Hills" reveals a questioning of grace, of the poetry of the head: such grace is undermined on the imaginative level. The simile points a finger at the symbol used and invites logic, reason, to destroy.

The simile leads to an extended metaphor, with the deer becoming the aristocrats facing the threat of revolution. Crichton Smith completes this composition of scene in the fifth stanza of this section:

> So were these deer, balanced on delicate logic,
> till suddenly they broke from us and went
> outraged and sniffing into the dark wind.[69]

"Balanced on delicate logic" offers a description of the way the deer walk but suggests too that it is a logic based on the poet's way of seeing. The deer turn and leave. They are "outraged." The anthropomorphism sits blatantly at the beginning of the line, descriptive, but containing within its meaning the awareness of the presumption of man's subjugating the animal kingdom with his perception. The poet's use of simile points up the disjunction between what is out there, and how the poet realises it for us. It is not "is" but "like"; the correspondence is oblique, not provable. The movement of his poem often leads to small moments of illumination. Crichton Smith still as it were places the fact-world in brackets, but here the process is somehow foregrounded. The text draws attention to its artificiality, the deliberateness of this meditative technique.

In section IV, Crichton Smith goes on to analyse his methods, to reject imposed, "idealist" modes of perception and to reject those moments of illumination which permeated his early work—perhaps especially that grace which removed him from the physical world, and death, towards sublimity: "Forget those purple evenings and these poems / that solved all."[70] The poet's language constructs his world. His language constructs the deer. In section V, a poetic manifesto emerges:

> You must build from the rain and stones,
> from the incurable numbers: the grasses
> innumerable on the many hills.
>
> Not to geometry or algebra,
> or an inhuman music, but
> in the hollow roar of the waterfall,
>
> you must build from there and not be
> circumvented by sunlight or a taste of love
> or intuitions from the sky above
>
> the deadly rock. Or even history,
> Prince Charles in a gay Highland shawl,
> or mystery in a black Highland coffin.
>
> You must build from the rain and stones
> till you can make
> a stylish deer on the high hills,
> and let its leaps be unpredictable![71]

There is a deliberate contrast between the imposition of his poetry on the world, and a drawing up and out of the world around him. "Build from there" gives him a starting point in the world, and not "intuitions from the sky above the deadly rock" inside his mind. The idealist is rejected and the imperative is towards a realist, or materialist, of the imagination. It is a poetic manifesto which rejects the persona of *The Long River* and poetry which is "inhuman music." "Incurable numbers," "grasses innumerable," celebrate the heterogeneity of the world, its escape from the mind which attempts to grasp it. It is the circle perpetually broken and transcended. Crichton Smith's explanation of his love of geometry usefully glosses "geometry or algebra" and "inhuman music":

Geometry appealed to some part of my nature which has to do with a love of order and elegance, and also to a part which has to do with a love of puzzle-solving. . . . The idea of elegance would later appear as the idea of grace. . . . For many years the poem to me was to be an elegant construction, not sweaty but pure, a musical artefact composed of exact language.[72]

"Elegant construction" describes neatly his poetry of geometric opposition. "Sweaty" is a complex description: I shall show in chapter six how "sweat" baptises the poet son. It is sufficient to note here that "pure" and "sweaty" offer two different poetries: the former a poetry of elegant construction, a poetry of the head, and the latter a poetry which is wrought on the imaginative level, and which takes the poet himself by surprise. Elegant geometry is rejected here. His twin poles are the sky above, and the deadly rock, the binaries of his poetry and the fact world. Here he finds an image of wide space, the sky, and the contained spaces of the grave, in the image of the gravestone, the "deadly rock." The rhyme of "history" and "mystery" places these two as parallel traps which threaten to circumvent the poet.

The last stanza in this section positions "make" at the end of a short line to highlight the multiple meanings of the word which offers us the sense of *maker* in its middle English sense of a poet who was a craftsman, not concerned with inspiration or originality but who practised a craft. There is also the sense that the poet wants the deer to be physically present, to make them appear as real as the actual. Both associations tug at the idea of creating images through poetry. The poet has created the deer for us at the beginning of the sequence but now he seems to want do do so in a new way. Yet it must be a deer just as "stylish." The last line, "let its leaps be unpredictable," presents layers of meaning. It means unpredictable in the sense of unexpected but on another level it has to do with "saying." The poet seems to want to create without that falseness, that obliqueness, of representation, to finally jump through that hoop of what he has described as "paper poems." Crichton Smith contemplates a way of writing which does not force his constructions on the world yet his construction of the deer as debutante or as Louis the Sixteenth in a self-conscious way defamiliarises both the deer and the act of seeing. Victor Shklovsky's definition of defamiliarisation sits easily with this poem: "Art exists that one may recover the sensation of life; it exists to make one feel things, to make the stone *stony*."[73] Crichton Smith too insists in section XIV, "There is no metaphor. The stone is stony."

In section VI, the poet Duncan Ban Macintyre is discussed as a man who could write poems about the deer, and yet shoot them. The deer of his imagination and the physical, wild animal were both kept separate and united by that bullet:

And the clean shot did not disturb his poems.
Nor did the deer kneel in a pool of tears.
The stakes were indeed high in that game.

And the rocks did not weep with sentiment.
They were simply there: the deer were simply there.
The witty gun blazed from his knowing hand.[74]

"The deer were simply there" echoes the opening of the second section.
The "witty gun" fuses the poetry with the killing. It establishes their
connection and their separation, the relationship of what seems the most
impossible, the relationship expressed in "beauty and brutality dance
together." Duncan Ban Macintyre is hailed as a man who could create
such a dance, who could view the object naked and yet be aware of the
distance between it and him.

Section VII explores that distance. These deer "inhabit wild systems."
The combination "wild systems" reveals the acknowledgement of that
otherness of the deer, compared to man's "churchyards, hotels or
schools" and yet reveals the difficulty of comprehending that otherness.
We see it still as system because that is the only way we can see it: "wild
systems" tugs constantly in opposite directions.

Crichton Smith offers a moment of analytical balance: "That halfway
kingdom is your royalty / you on a meditative truth impaled."[75] The
lines continue the terms of sovereignty and revolution yet the halfway
kingdom is also the moment of analytical balance, of seeing the deer
naked yet distant. They are symbol, and wild animal, part of the fact
world indifferent to his poetry.

In section XIII, the symbol is scrutinised:

Are rivers stories, and are plains their prose?
Are fountains poetry? And are rainbows the
wistful smiles upon a dying face?[76]

The enjambment here after the staccato questions gives a sense of crisis.
Meditation leads to the discovery that both world and language alienate:
"are you a world away, a language distant? / Such symbols freeze upon
my desolate lips!"[77] Accepting such isolation, the language twists and
bends: the poet's condemnation of metaphor whisks us back to the
ballroom:

There is no metaphor. The stone is stony.
The deer step out in isolated air.
We move at random on an innocent journey.[78]

"Step out" leads us back to the debutantes in the ballroom. The journey
is a metaphor for life. The words cannot stay pure. The poet becomes
an Orphic figure:

46

> So being lonely I would speak with any
> stone or tree or river. Bear my journey
> you endless water, dance with a human joy.[79]

"Bear my journey / you endless water" is a phrase which evokes the metaphors of Crichton Smith's poetry. His first volume was entitled *The Long River*, a metaphor for the writing of poetry. He has spoken of community as offering buoyancy.[80] Shimmering there too is an image of suicide by drowning. As the poet writes "there is no metaphor" he lies. If all language is metaphoric, still he has silence left. Yet silence is death for the poet. The next stanza swings to the images of Keats's "Ode On A Grecian Urn" as if in a moment of panic:

> This distance deadly! God or goddess throw me
> a rope to landscape, let that hill, so bare,
> blossom with grapes, the wine of Italy.[81]

Distance may be deadly, but so too is that landscape. The "hill, so bare" is a world very much like the bare Calvinist world of Lewis where the young boy's wooden hens were rejected as graven images. The allusion to Keats's poem is an instinctive movement towards the "vase" of his own poetry, a movement from what is threatening, from death, towards that other world in which he can flourish.

"Deer On The High Hills" closes with a return to an incantation of recalcitrant reality:

> for stars are starry and the rain is rainy,
> the stone is stony and the sun is sunny,
> the deer step out in isolated air.[82]

Yet that "for" lifts it away from a reality which threatens silence towards something positive, something that will not destroy his poetry but supply the catalyst for new work. There is no naked object. The creative aspect of perception will always blur the separation between subject and object. The meditation explores the binaries of the animal world and the world of men. Crichton Smith admired "On A Raised Beach" because it was:

> a poem about stones and an appalling apartness. It is in this kind of conscious loneliness that MacDiarmid is most imaginatively convincing. . . . It is the aristocratic, lonely voice in these poems that convinces.[83]

The meditation's discovery is that the deer are twice distant: a world and a language apart. The aristocratic, lonely voice is Crichton Smith's, too.

The definition of the early poetry as a poetry of opposition is a useful starting point. The poet is able to separate a closed, written history from a free, created self, and to find an achieved identity, a state of grace. Yet it is a poetry of movement: the self is negotiated somewhere between these oppositions. "Deer On The High Hills" offers us two poets: the poet of *The Long River* whose poetry was marked by brilliant imagery, striking metaphor, a subject in splendid isolation, and a new poet emerging, the poet of the later volumes for whom such isolation is a false state of grace. Here is a transitional stage, a poet looking back to the poetry of his early career, and looking forward to a poetry which threatens to lead to silence.

Notes

1. J. H. Alexander, "The English Poetry of Iain Crichton Smith," in *Literature of the North*, edited by David Hewitt and Michael Spiller (Aberdeen: Aberdeen University Press, 1983), pp. 189-203 (p. 192); Roderick Watson, "Scottish Poetry 1981," *Studies in Scottish Literature*, 19 (1981), 208-215 (p. 208).
2. John Blackburn, "A Writer's Journey," booklet and five cassette recordings (Edinburgh: Moray House College of Education, 1981).
3. *The Complete Poems of Hugh MacDiarmid*, Vol. 1, edited by M. Grieve and W. R. Aitken (London: Penguin, 1985), p. 87.
4. G. Gregory Smith, *Scottish Literature* (London: Macmillan, 1919).
5. Ronnie Turnbull and Craig Beveridge, "R. D. Laing and Scottish Philosophy," *New Edinburgh Review*, 78-9 (1988), 119-128 (p. 120).
6. *Ibid.*
7. Billy Kay, "The Incurable Disease Called Writing," talk given at the Bonar Hall, Dundee, May 5, 1990.
8. "My Relationship With Poetry," *Chapman*, 16, 4:4 (Summer 1976), 12-18 (pp. 14-15).
9. Interview with Iain Crichton Smith, Taynuilt, 1987.
10. *The Long River* (Edinburgh: Macdonald, 1955), p. 9.
11. *Ibid.*
12. *Ibid.*, p. 22.
13. *The Complete Poems of Hugh MacDiarmid*, p. 240.
14. *The Long River*, p. 23.
15. *Ibid.*, p. 14.
16. *Ibid.*, p. 20.
17. "Between Sea and Moor" in *As I Remember*, edited by Maurice Lindsay (London: Hale, 1979), pp. 107-121 (p. 118).
18. *The Long River*, p. 13.
19. "My Relationship With Poetry," p. 18.
20. *The Long River*, p. 15.
21. *Ibid.*, p. 16.
22. *Ibid.*, p. 11.
23. *Ibid.*
24. "An American Sky," in *The Black And The Red and Other Stories* (London: Gollancz, 1973), p. 63.
25. *As I Remember*, pp. 118-119.
26. *Selected Poems 1955-80*, edited by Robin Fulton (Edinburgh: Macdonald, 1981), p. 4.

27. Lorn Macintyre, "Poet in Bourgeois Land," *Scottish International*, 25 (1971), 22-27 (p. 23).
28. Iain H. Murray (editor), *The Diary of Kenneth MacRae* (Edinburgh: Banner of Truth Trust, 1980), p. 264.
29. *As I Remember*, p. 116.
30. ",Poet in Bourgeois Land," p. 24.
31. *The Law and the Grace*, p. 16.
32. *Ibid.*
33. *Ibid.*, p. 17.
34. *Ibid.*, p. 16.
35. "*Collected Poems* by George Bruce," in *Lines Review*, 36 (March 1971), 39-40 (p. 39).
36. *New Poets*, edited by Edwin Muir (London: Eyre & Spottiswoode, 1959), p. 20.
37. *Ibid.*
38. *Ibid.*, p. 21.
39. *The Law and the Grace*, p. 22.
40. *Ibid.*, p. 19.
41. *Thistles and Roses*, p. 14.
42. *Ibid.*
43. Carol Gow, "An Interview with Iain Crichton Smith," *Scottish Literary Journal* 17:2 (November 1990), 43-57 (p. 45).
44. *Thistles and Roses*, p. 41.
45. *Towards The Human* (Edinburgh: Macdonald, 1986), p. 23.
46. "'Nine to four' Classroom Vanished Long Ago," *The Scotsman*, 20 August 1985, p. 20.
47. *Ibid.*
48. *The Law and the Grace*, p. 31.
49. *Ibid.*, p. 23.
50. *Ibid.*, p. 44.
51. *Consider the Lilies* (London: Gollancz, 1968), p. 27.
52. *Ibid.*, p. 169.
53. *Thistles and Roses*, p. 12.
54. *Ibid.*, pp. 47-48.
55. *Ibid.*, p. 34.
56. *Ibid.*, p. 33.
57. *Ibid.*, p. 9.
58. *Ibid.*
59. *Ibid.*, pp. 22-23.
60. *Ibid.*, p. 22.
61. "The Golden Lyric," in *Hugh MacDiarmid: A Critical Survey*, edited by Duncan Glen (London: Chatto & Windus, 1972), pp. 124-140 (p. 138).
62. Introduction to translation of *Ben Dòrain* (Preston: Akros, 1969), p. 4.
63. *Ibid.*, p. 7.
64. *Deer On The High Hills* (Edinburgh: Giles Gordon, 1962), I.
65. "MacDiarmid and Ideas, with special reference to 'On A Raised Beach'" in *The Age of MacDiarmid: Essays on Hugh MacDiarmid and his influence on contemporary Scotland*, edited by P. H. Scott and A. C. Davis (Edinburgh: Mainstream, 1980). pp. 157-162 (p. 161).
66. *The Long River* (Edinburgh: Macdonald, 1955), p. 14.
67. *Deer On The High Hills*, II.
68. I. Kant, *The Critique of Judgement*, translated by J. C. Meredith (London: Clarendon, 1969), p. 170.
69. *Deer On The High Hills*, II.
70. *Ibid.*, IV.
71. *Ibid.*, V.

D

72. *As I Remember*, p. 112.
73. Lee T. Lemon and Marion J. Reis, *Russian Formalist Criticism: Four Essays* (Nebraska: Nebraska University Press, 1965), p. 12.
74. *Deer On The High Hills*, VI.
75. *Ibid.*, XII.
76. *Ibid.*, XIII.
77. *Ibid.*
78. *Ibid.*, XIV.
79. *Ibid.*
80. *Towards the Human*, p. 24.
81. *Deer On The High Hills*, XIV.
82. *Ibid.*
83. *Hugh MacDiarmid: A Critical Survey*, p. 132.

CHAPTER THREE

Hamlet

If the Gaelic Matriarch is delineated again and again in an act of cleansing, an act which attempts to separate the poet from the time and place in which he was born, Crichton Smith's identification of a Scottish cultural stereotype suggests a similar strategy: elucidating and clarifying the discourses of the Scottish church, the education system and the media, he reveals how a concept of "Scottishness" is inscribed in the language these institutions perpetuate. For the poet living and writing in Scotland, for the Scots people themselves, Crichton Smith suggests, being born at a certain time in a certain place makes a Scottish identity problematic: the mirror offered reflects a tired, bourgeois cultural stereotype. Strangling the last minister with the last copy of *The Sunday Post* is not enough. Crichton Smith sees a couthy "Scottishness" as a real evil which threatens to destroy individuality, and yet which cannot wholly be identified as other: it is inscribed in our discourse, it is in the air we breathe. Kailyardism, for Crichton Smith, like his Calvinism, is a state of mind.

Ian Campbell offers us a useful definition of Kailyardism as

> a gelling of attitude and myth, a freezing of the possibilities of change and redefinition, a tacit acceptance of a narrow range of character and activity within which to present "real" Scotland; above all, a total weakness in any attempt to challenge the reader into startling or threatening identification or redefinition.[1]

It became fashionable to reject the Kailyard: George Douglas Brown's *The House With The Green Shutters*, published in 1901, reacted against "the sentimental slop of Barrie, and Crockett, and Maclaren," the novels of the Kailyard which sentimentalised country life and which crystallised a couthy Scottishness. Brown's novel insisted the boundaries be redrawn.[2] For Crichton Smith, however, the Kailyard is not a certain kind of literature which can be rewritten, but is entangled and intertwined with our ideas of what being "Scots" is all about. Ian Campbell makes the point neatly when he argues for the essential values of the Kailyard school:

> The Kailyarders invited pride in a Scottish Church, social fabric, educational system and historical sense which no Scot in the 1980s would wish to reject, grossly as it may be parodied. To reject the Kailyard is to reject much that is central to any attempt to define "Scottishness."[3]

If Ian Campbell comes close to suggesting that "Scottishness" is almost defined—and confined—by the Kailyard, Crichton Smith is quite prepared to throw the baby out with the bathwater.

Perhaps unsurprisingly, therefore, the volume which most centrally tackles "Scottishness," *From Bourgeois Land*, published in 1969, was criticised as showing "some failure of imagination and sensitivity" in a contemporary review.[4] There is no doubt that in experimenting with the language of his poetry here, in attempting to root it firmly in a time and a place by taking up the language of Bourgeois Land, Crichton Smith relinquishes much that vitalises his work: the unexpected collocation, the startling image, the movement of wheeling, evolving meaning. Certainly here are poems which rate amongst his best work. In poem 17, for example, "The wind roars," the movement, the images, the tragic resolution, are all distinctively Crichton Smith's. And in poem 34 he finds an image which is one of the most memorable he has ever written: "the hammered poetry of Dante turns / light as a wristwatch, bright as a thousand suns." Yet there are other poems in which the poetry is sacrificed for comment or argument and the result is often one of an impromptu response: many of the poems lack metrical interest and are linguistically drab. There is no doubt that criticism of the volume as distinctly uneven is justified. But the volume's timing perhaps invited a rather hostile response. Here was a poet denouncing Scotland and at a time when there seemed to be a growing sense of national pride. Crichton Smith's comments in 1981 suggest why he seemed out of step:

> Take the Referendum . . . on that particular day I thought, "Is it possible to commit yourself to the new, to make a leap into the new?" And I felt—I feel all the time that there isn't enough of this leap. It's just talking about what has gone on in the past.[5]

Yet Crichton Smith's impatience with a Scottish *ennui* belies the discoveries of his poetry. The binaries offered in the comment above are the new and the past. The poet establishes a similar set of binaries in "The Temptation," a poem from the *Thistles and Roses* collection, but suggests that such oppositions are simplistic. "Imagine" and "Remember" form the twin temptations in a *psychomachia* which tempts both poet and reader towards a sacerdotal perfection. Like the new and the past, imagine and remember offer simple binaries which can no longer be tolerated by the poet. The last few lines of "The Temptation" crystalise into an image of internal conflict, revealing a man "bent in two / to teach him that his arrows must fly true."[6] The "leap" into the new, the escape from the past is not the answer. As Scots, we have to come to terms with the past, and to find out how to live *now*.

Crichton Smith's zealous attack on the "wha's like us" mentality, however, may stem from the fact that he freely admits that once he "lived in a kingdom of the wish, as the poets of the kailyard did." An avid football fan, he recalls that he listened to the radio and annually heard the Scots team being beaten by England. He admits, "*in spite of the facts*, I always considered Scotland to be a better football team than England." The kingdom of the wish is the trap laid in "The Temptation" of "imagine" untested by "remember" and facilitates the creation of a mythic Scotland

> which had the first good democratic education system, of a Scotland which had the first good football teams, of a Scotland which had the first good shipyards. . . . Either we boasted of our great Scottish inventors or we looked back to the "house in the glen," or both. In any case we refused to face reality; our literature of the kailyard seemed to be saying that all things Scottish were good (and we inherited this idea from the chauvinistic side of Burns) and that all we had to do was live with the simplicity of our forefathers.[7]

Fleeing the kailyard means abandoning the luggage of the past in order to make that leap into the new. "The Temptation" reveals why the leap into the new is impossible. The leap is the movement by which the past, the written history, is escaped. It is the movement of the poetry in *The Long River* which posits a created, written self. It is the leap the poet admires in MacDiarmid's poetry, and in the jokes of the Goons: an imaginative leap which frees itself from reality and logic. Crichton Smith's hesitation about that leap is significant. The movement towards a more complex statement was prefigured in "Deer On The High Hills" with "Forget these purple evenings and those poems / that solved all" and in the poem, "Whether Beyond the Stormy Hebrides":

> Too simple an ending that,
> that he should rise as the sun rises
> out of the waters where it never set.
> Too simple this pure art's hypothesis
> transforming bones and flesh into light.[8]

In his early poems, identity for the poet was "the diamond-browed one" in a world beyond this world. In his poems about Scotland, Crichton Smith adopts the identities of Hamlet or Kierkegaard and walks abroad in bourgeois Scotland. It is a move from counter-identification to disidentification. The movement shows a desire to establish a persona set in time and place—even though that time and place is hostile. *From Bourgeois Land* finds little favour with critics not just because it was seen as an attack on "Scottishness" but perhaps because in his exploration of language and ideology, in his hesitation and suspicion of metaphor, Crichton Smith's poetry becomes uneven here, too often losing its mystery and fascination and becoming flat. It has been remarked that Crichton Smith is an uneven poet: perhaps that is true of all poets who write and publish a large body of work. Yet when poems do fail, it seems to me they are honest failures: born of a poet who relentlessly pursues and explores the paths he opens up, and does so publicly. Always, with Crichton Smith, one senses that he too is reader of his own work. *From Bourgeois Land*, then, contains honest failures perhaps because the discoveries made limit the poetic power: setting himself down in a certain place at a certain time too often silences the "diamond-browed one" of the early poetry.

We are all constructed in and by our language, by the time and place in which we are born. "Imagine" and "Remember" are the twin temptations in a *psychomachia* which dramatises not just the poet's dilemma, but the dilemma of all Scots. "Imagine" has been rejected by the poet because without a past, a history, he has no identity. Yet that past, that history, is hostile. Infiltrating the Kailyard as spy, the poet is able to construct an identity in a certain place at a certain time, yet to remain the stranger. King Lear sees himself and Cordelia as "Gods' spies," as if reporting on the activities of men.[9] There is certainly the sense of the visitor reporting on another world in *From Bourgeois Land*, but perhaps more usefully "spy" suggests something of Kierkegaard's method of observation:

> Even if the world at large was alien, even if it was "unintelligible" and "infected," this did not mean that it could not be utilised. For if one kept one's eyes open, if one did not become too closely involved in it, but viewed it with the slightly quizzical gaze of the scientist inspecting a new specimen, if one did all this, then the world could become a rich source of anecdotes, psychological aperçus, and suggestive ideas. It need only be *observed*.[10]

In *From Bourgeois Land*, the poet adopts the personae of Kierkegaard and Hamlet to provide identity, a cover, which protects him in an alien land. These choices are revealing: both are chosen as poets, both are isolated within a community. Crichton Smith's interest in Kierkegaard hinges on the relationship between the individual and community:

> It's very hard, I think, to make poetry and to make oneself, and I think one of the . . . people who comes into my mind with regard to this particular aspect is Kierkegaard. Now for a long, long period I was very, very interested in Kierkegaard's philosophy . . . it may have been partly the idea of someone who's within a relatively small community in Copenhagen but at the same time is outwith the community. But also . . . Kierkegaard I think was also a poet as well as a philosopher and . . . one of the ideas that I got from Kierkegaard was that we have to try to make ourselves into individuals.[11]

It is interesting to note how much the individual is seen as under construction here, despite the constant battle in the poetry between ideas of self-construction and the self who can only ever be a product of his society. Kierkegaard offers a useful role model for the poet at this stage because Kierkegaard suggests that the conflict between "imagine" and "remember," between the creation of a self and the written history, can be resolved. In Crichton Smith's poem, "Kierkegaard," unity is created from division:

> Tragedy? or Comedy? These meet
> in the written mirrors furnishing his chill
> and flashing Danish room. . . .
>
> Till the new category, the individual,
> rose like a thorn from the one rose he knew.[12]

And how close Crichton Smith seems to Kierkegaard in "Statement By A Responsible Spinster" whose statement in turn describes the poet: "I inspect justice through a queer air."[13]

Crichton Smith's fascination with Hamlet, too, is bound up with the individual within a community:

> He seems to me to represent the vulnerable intellectual and poet, since I think of him as a poet. He also represents the complexity of the fine mind which sees so many points of view that it becomes paralysed. Also he uses language like a god.
>
> The spy connection is because of the continual spying on him in the castle, the endless images of curtains etc. It would be too much to say it links with growing up in a closed community but maybe there is something in that. He is fighting to be himself, but people are always trying to find his "secret."[14]

Like Crichton Smith, Kierkegaard and Hamlet wrestle with being situated in a certain place at a certain time. For both, Denmark is an alien place. Kierkegaard's use of "infected" neatly illuminates the basic opposition Crichton Smith senses in his Calvinist background: an opposition linked through imagery of TB to death. The Calvinist self is set on a journey towards death, Thanatos. For Hamlet, poet, courtier, prince, corrupt Denmark smells of mortality: though he "uses language like a god," none of the roles he creates saves him from his tragic fate. The part written for him must be played out; the dénouement is fixed.

Bourgeois Scotland is Crichton Smith's Denmark. His poems about Scotland of the late 60s and early 70s are not the poems beloved of nationalists or dewy-eyed exiles. He saw little around him to challenge his comment in 1971 that Scotland as a country was "dedicated to the second rate":[15]

> Very often I feel ashamed of Scotland. We have to pick ourselves up from the ground all the time. We get beaten in everything. . . . I just want Scotland to produce something that I would consider excellent. Well, what have they produced—MacDiarmid's poetry, and Celtic Football Club—in the past 30 years perhaps?[16]

For Crichton Smith, MacDiarmid is "an exemplar of what is humanly possible, as a concept of excellence and persistence"—and Celtic had just won the European Cup.[17] The slide from "we" to "they" in the quotation above reveals a poet for whom isolation is an instinctive position. "Excellent," "excellence and persistence," find their echo in the rallying call in "The White Air of March": "Excellence! / 'Costing not less than everything'."[18] Excellence is the opposition to the stultifying Kailyard. If Ian Campbell singles out the church, the social fabric, the education system and the historical sense as a source of pride, Crichton Smith singles these out, too, but in order to reveal them as powers which crush individuality and eccentricity, which perpetuate a dead stereotype. Against the "simplicity of our forefathers" Crichton Smith sets the "infinitely complex."[19]

"Scotland," "By The Sea" and "The White Air of March" describe a Scotland of golfing provosts, of ragged pipers, The White Heather Club and The Sunday Post. In "The White Air of March" the poet depicts a local press steeped in the parochial, reporting mind-numbing trivia as news and he foregrounds that favourite caption, "a shared joke":

> Have you not seen
> the glossy weddings in the glossy pages,
> champagne and a "shared joke."[20]

Crichton Smith has written of spending his school lunchtimes in Stornoway library, "reading magazines like the Tatler bound in leather covers and seeing pictures of the aristocracy bound together by a 'common joke'."[21] "Bound in leather covers," "bound together" and "common joke" offer metaphors for the community and a shared ideology. Yet that word "joke" is a slippery one in this poet's vocabulary. Both the *Tatler* and his local press are involved in a reinforcing of identity: the one a metropolitan, class-bound, upper-crust community, the other the "bourgeois" community of Scotland. Both seek to define, and the poet suggests, confine, too. Crichton Smith's churchmen are portrayed as parochial and inward-looking through their choice of Sunday newspaper: "Let us put aside the *Observer*, let us remember / the invocations of the *Sunday Post*."[22] The title of the newspaper cast aside takes on new significance in the light of the spy persona of *From Bourgeois Land* and Sunday is a day of observance. These connotations of the act of seeing serve only to suggest myopia. Sales of *The Sunday Post* have remained at saturation point in Scotland for many years: it is the traditional newspaper. In many ways it is recognised as a "joke," to borrow Crichton Smith's word. A comedy sketch on BBC television showed the Scots actor Rikki Fulton walking into a newsagent's shop and buying openly and confidently a selection of pornographic literature—only to become sly and shifty as he whispered a last request for "The Sunday Post" which was bundled quickly into a brown paper bag.[23] We may regard *The Sunday Post* with affection and relegate it to the realms of Tartanry along with shortbread and the jokey postcards, yet the newspaper has a great deal of power in how it reflects "Scottishness" to Scottish people themselves and to people abroad. It offers up a picture of Scotland as decent, law-abiding and church-going, and yet a Scotland which is never nationalistic but wedded firmly and affectionately to England.

To the poet, Tartanry, the Kailyard, is not something easily identifiable as other, but is inscribed in the language in which we as Scots are constructed. In *From Bourgeois Land*, Crichton Smith attempts to expose that language, to reveal how it works. As poet, he attempts to liberate our language and therefore our identities as Scots to allow for complexity, plurality and multiplicity. Tackling the spectre of Tartanry, the poet places himself at risk. No longer aloof and isolated, he attempts to work within the discourses of Scotland and win back territory. The uneasiness of the poet's position is implicit in the very texture of the poetry itself, in the degree of imaginative failure. It is made explicit in "The White Air of March," a kind of Scottish "The Wasteland": the quotation in "Excellence! / 'costing not less than everything'" comes from Eliot's *Four Quartets*; he alludes to other writers as if in need of reassurance, community. If in "Calling the Roll" in *The Long River* the young poet reached out instinctively towards English writers, he reaches out to international minds here:

I speak now of those who told the truth.
Let them be praised.
Dostoyevsky, Nietzsche, Kierkegaard,
Kafka—let them be honoured.[24]

Here are national writers claimed by their countries, but the truth for them rises above nationality. Explaining this group, Crichton Smith seems to be thinking in terms of the confining circle:

> People who actually go forward as individuals, and are willing to test themselves to their own limits intensely, and none of them have [sic] what I would call the kind of bourgeois consciousness which prevents us from getting anywhere.[25]

The need to free himself from what he perceives as a bourgeois community, and the need to root his poems in a firm reality, conflict in "The White Air of March." The poem ends "In the white air of March / a new mind" and offers the nervous leap, the claim for transcendence, made by the earlier poet.[26] But the challenge has not been met squarely. Crichton Smith's exploration of Scottishness in *From Bourgeois Land* confronts more closely the gap which that leap denies.

If Hamlet personifies excellence in Bourgeois Land, his opposite is an Eichmann figure. In the first poem in this collection, the poet attempts the description of an ordinary, sober, clerk just doing his job. But "bourgeois" progresses steadily to mean damned:

> But otherwise, you clerk who hated error
> more than the sin that yet involves us all,
> I say, "You are so monstrous I would call
> the bells of hell, gassed faces in the mirror,
> to enliven age on age your bourgeois soul."[27]

The poet here links evil with the self-righteous, the parochial, mind untroubled by imagination or bad dreams. That kind of mentality can commit atrocities as part of a job, obediently, systematically. Evil is undramatic and ordinary, so ordinary that it threatens to involve us all. Hannah Arendt's portrayal of Eichmann argued for the "banality of evil." She described Eichmann's language; the "officialese" which was his only means of expression, the "language rule" in which bald words like "extermination" were amended to "final solution." Arendt suggests that Eichmann's incapacity for ordinary speech, his inability to express himself other than in clichés, made him an ideal candidate for language rules. Defending her term, "the banality of evil," she said:

> when I speak of the banality of evil, I do so only on the strictly factual level, pointing to a phenomenon which stared one in the face

at the trial. Eichmann was not Iago and not Macbeth, and nothing would have been farther from his mind than to determine with Richard III "to prove a villain.". . . He *merely . . . never realised what he was doing.*[28]

Crichton Smith, like Arendt, recognises the banality of evil, but his uncharacteristic response at the end of this poem testifies to its power. His "clerk" is "monstrous." His fight to liberate the language in which "Scottishness" is inscribed is drawn on a sombre stage: it is serious drama. The lack of imagination, the lack of a language, allowed Eichmann to fulfil his function within Nazi Germany. Ian Campbell's definition of Kailyardism included "a total weakness in any attempt to challenge the reader into startling or threatening identification or redefinition," Crichton Smith's linking of Bourgeois Land and Nazi Germany displays no such weakness but a shocking boldness. If MacDiarmid's "A Drunk Man Looks At The Thistle" burst on the Scottish consciousness like childbirth in church, *From Bourgeios Land* offers a shocking picture of Kaiser in the Kailyard and though it is not the most admired of Crichton Smith's volumes, it will surely mark a watershed in our perception of "Scottishness."

The volume was seen as equating "Calvinist Protestantism with the rise of capitalism, and capitalism in turn with totalitarian ideology and practice."[29] The connection may be shocking, but it is not new— Crichton Smith pointed out that R. H. Tawney equates Calvinism and capitalism in *Religion and the Rise of Capitalism.*[30] The German-Frankfurt school recognised a similar connection.[31] Erich Fromm argued that Luther and Calvin prepared man for his role as "servant to the economic machine"—and eventually a "Fuhrer."[32] Crichton Smith is in line with this response, which many more recent historians may feel is a little too simplistic. What his portrayal of "bourgeois" reveals is the desperate need to push the poet and his community to extremes. The movement towards establishing the individual within a community is countered by establishing the individual and the community at their extreme opposites, lest the poet discover the distinctions blur. His choice of Hamlet is interesting here: in many ways, Hamlet is a very "bourgeois" choice, revealing that the "bourgeois" quality he seeks to escape may not be entirely other. The figure of Hamlet continues to fascinate Crichton Smith throughout his work: Hamlet as tragic hero is sufficiently complex to allow for a continuing exploration of tragedy, absurdity and farce.

Crichton Smith's extreme response to his Gaelic inheritance, to Highland Scotland, reveals an awareness of its power. How can the individual who has been raised in a Gaelic culture, and always lived in Scotland, escape his time and place? The ideology of a community is not something "out there" that can be accepted or rejected: it is inscribed in its discourses. It is "the very condition of our experience of the world, *un*conscious precisely in that it is unquestioned, taken for granted."[33]

The Scottishness" that Crichton Smith identifies is created through language. Examining the language of the press, the church, the Scottish people themselves, he can defamiliarise the construction, prise open the boundaries. The attempt to create his own language, to reject the discourses he has been offered, is fraught with difficulties. That is why as "spy" set down in Bourgeois Land, he creates for himself the protective skins of his literary personae, that is why he constantly breaks the boundaries of meaning and opens up discourse to multiple meanings. Through complexity, multiplicity and chaos, he attempts to escape the constrictions of time and place, the discourse he is offered which confines and defines. The earlier "The Law and The Grace" works with these oppositions. The pressure from the community is to conform: "We know no angels. If you say you do / that's blasphemy and devilry." Rejecting their idea of theological grace, a grace he sees as won through distortion and ugliness, the poet finds grace in its opposite. The poetry, too, achieves that effortless grace characteristic of Crichton Smith's work, and if it is separated, protected from time and place, yet it offers a confident, sure poetry:

> No, I have angels. Mine
> are free and perfect. They have no design
> on anyone else, but only on my pride
>
> my insufficiency, imperfect works.
> They often leave me, but they sometimes come
> to judge me to the core, till I am dumb.
> Is this not law enough, you patriarchs?[34]

The poet as spy or Hamlet still denies the patriarch, the fatherland, the father figure and the forefathers but he attempts to develop from the simplicities of neat opposition, of setting law against art, the direct confrontation, and works stealthily, reclaiming territory. He is aware of the power of the opposition which is strong enough to appropriate even the strongest of figures in Scottish literature—Burns. Burns is claimed as a "genius" and "an ordinary person":

> "Ah such a genius," the church intones.
> "Such love of justice and equality.
> An ordinary person just like us.
> Flesh of our flesh, bones of our very bones.
> A genius walking under an Ayrshire sky."[35]

The "genius" is the celebrity who has gained fame and respect in the larger world outside Scotland. Yet his countrymen know he is "just like us," and so share vicariously in his success. By denying his difference, and accentuating his ordinariness, his individual success, his standing out from his community, is punished. Like the Calvinist community of Lewis, here individual success unrelated to community is suspect. *Cliù* appertains only to those who conform to the standards and ideals of society. In Lewis, a celebrity who was morally tainted would not have *cliù*. Yet the church here will not relinquish its claim to bask in the reflected glory of Burns, even if he was a sinner. They choose to see Burns's exceptional talent as reflecting the community in which he was born. His morals are seen as objectionable but can be generously—and neatly—separated from his distinction:

> He may have sinned. Which of us hasn't sinned?
> But which of us has left such gems behind him?
> So therefore let us toast him, wife and hubby,
> giving thanks to God for the treasure of his mind.[36]

The words "gems," "wife and hubby," are petty bourgeois words which show the way his genius is claimed and inscribed in their language. The last two stanzas in the poem bring a very distinctive "poetic" discourse to oppose the words spoken by the church—a discourse which is distinctive not just of Crichton Smith but of Burns, too. Heaven, God and Eden are invoked as the bourgeois language is overpowered by the brilliance of lines which deny constriction and limitation in various ways. Lack of definition is insisted upon by the use of "somewhere" and "varying," and the rules of grammar are reworked by using abstractions as concrete nouns in "you touched her breasts to brilliant inspiration" and "her naked legs spun stanzas." The poem itself removes Burns from the narrow confines of the church and into the open, windy countryside, from the circle to freedom outside the circle just as Crichton Smith's poetry seems to free itself from statement and logic and take a characteristic imaginative leap.

In "Church," however, the poet is not content simply to set his discourse in opposition, but instead reworks the discourse of his bourgeois church, revealing a shrewd business-sense, cynical and calculating:

> God must mean
> success and harmony, his dividends
> are still increasing and to get your share
> all that you need is faith. His interests are
> world-wide and deep.[37]

"Dividends" plays on "divine" and the puns on "share" and "interest" invest these terms with straight economic values. The parables in the

Bible frequently use the language of buying and selling in order to illuminate. Here metaphoric use of language is confined to "must mean," and rigidly defined. God's works are economic works. Death is seen in terms of redundancy, an economic necessity: "till the purge / of useless workmen will appease his pique."[38] The poem is an interesting one, but works less well, perhaps, than "At The Sale." This too reveals a discourse based on economic terms, but finds that pulse point which makes it not just interesting, but inspiring, too.

"At The Sale" shows a nation, humanity itself, judged in economic terms. The poem deals ostensibly with the bric-à-brac of an auction sale but the images are carefully chosen and become symbols. Objects of a home and an old hierarchy are heaped together in disorder:

> Old beds, old chairs, old mattresses, old books,
> old pictures of coiffed women, hatted men,
> ministers with clamped lips and flowing beards,
> a Duke in his Highland den.[39]

"Clamped lips" (an image which invites comparison with the "set mouth" of his old woman and the smiling lips of his schoolgirl in *Thistles and Roses*) belong to the Presbyterian ministers at the time of The Clearances, who, in a position of authority, gave the Highlanders no guidance or help, as Crichton Smith portrays Mr Brown betraying those who trusted to the church in *Consider the Lilies*. They are also the symbol of the Puritanism of disapproval. Scattered among all these are shepherd's crooks, a symbol of the sheep for whom the land was cleared. The bric-à-brac represents a way of life uprooted and discarded, sold for profit.

The middle movement of the poem deals with the procedures of the sale. The auctioneer has "quick eyes" which "swoop on a glance, a half-seen movement" like some bird of prey, Scotland its victim. The third movement begins with another piece of bric-à-brac, and describes an old machine, but the word which begins the fourth line of the fifth stanza is "imagine" and it pushes the reading of the poem unambiguously towards extended metaphor as that outdated and outcast machine becomes a symbol for the redundancy of self:

> Imagine how we will
> endlessly pump and turn for forty years
> and then receive a pension, smart and clean.[40]

The objects discarded in the first part of the poem were part of a way of life, warmed by human hands. This machine, wrenched from its once-productive context, is meaningless. "What's this object for?" It is now a "nameless gadget." The last lines remain truthful to the context of an auction sale but the word "appalling" contains the idea of pall and shroud, turning this place into hell and involving us all in the discourse of the poet:

> O hold me, love, in this appalling place.
> Let your hand stay me by this mattress here
> and this tall ruined glass,
> by this dismembered radio, this queer
> machine that waits and has no history.[41]

The "ruined glass" and the "dismembered radio" represent a dead culture, the mirror reflecting nothing, the radio silenced. What remains is the machine which has "no history" because it has no words with which to record that history. Crichton Smith offers a vision of a life with no past to sustain it, in a country where, after the Clearances, he has suggested, history was wiped away.

What remains is parody, caricature. Writing up the past, we appropriate it in our bourgeois discourse. In "Dido and Aeneas," the poet allows his imagined audience to condemn themselves when he submits Virgil's story to their popular Scottish press. The desertion is inevitable and commendable to the bourgeois mind which reads the story as one of duty, responsibility, the subjugation of the individual to community:

> Accord him honour, he had work to do,
> set up committees, build his marble halls,
> train a Civil Service and install
> a vulgar praetor of a parvenu.[42]

He is a "good sound man, a patriarch of the town." Aeneas, the poet's own tragic hero, triumphs here as someone very like a good prospective provost or town councillor. In *The Last Summer* there is a classroom discussion of Virgil's poem. Crichton Smith's hero, Malcolm, sees no virtue in Aeneas. I have already made clear the close connection between the hero of this novel and the young Crichton Smith. Malcolm dismisses the argument that Aeneas had his duty to do:

> "Fascist," said Malcolm suddenly. "What do you think we're fighting for. Isn't that what Hitler says, that the race is more important than the individual? . . . And furthermore I would like to ask what kind of Rome would be founded by an Aeneas who could do that kind of thing?"[43]

The classroom discussion explores the rational and the irrational, the individual versus community. Each contributor offers a partial solution, but the text defers judgement and shows that the tragic meaning of Virgil's poem partakes of all these interpretations. In this way, the writer avoids making a statement, because "to offer a constructive solution is not the kind of thing that a poet does."[44] The meaning of Virgil's tragedy cannot be defined simply: the meaning of "Scottishness" can be explored and widened, but definition would confine.

Crichton Smith's poetry is always personal and private. His voice is not usually a public one, but almost a decade after the publication of *From Bourgeois Land* he wrote a poem in response to a controversial speech by the Reverend Angus Smith, Moderator of the General Assembly of the Free Church of Scotland in 1986. In "After Reading The Speech By The Rev Angus Smith, Parts of Which Were Reported in 'The West Highland Free Press'," the poet picks up the tone of the speech and some of the vocabulary to expose the ideology:

> Let the pages of the Bible open like the wings of vultures.
> In Northern Ireland, in South Africa,
> there is not enough killing: in
> Glasgow there is as yet only shadow-boxing.[45]

In his speech, the Reverend Smith catalogued the grants from the World Council of Churches awarded to the combating of racism. Most of the money he says was aimed against South Africa and apartheid, he suggests, because "South Africa's real crime is that she is Calvinistic, with praying members in her cabinet. Marxist liberation movements bent on violence seem to be the main beneficiaries of the fund." On the Irish situation and the Orange Order, the Reverend Smith observed, "We do not have the siege mentality which obtains in Northern Ireland where the Order is much more virile and Protestants better informed. The Protestant-Catholic conflict in Scotland today is only shadow-boxing."[46] *From Bourgeois Land* surely finds new illumination and some vindication in the light of this speech. It is unusual for Crichton Smith to take a public or political stance. The impetus for the poem above came from the same hatred of the exercise of power that prompted *From Bourgeois Land*: "there are things . . . I still feel quite angry about, things like apartheid and any form of people trying to impose power on other people."[47]

The poet, a private voice, does not seek power. In "Speaker," the poet ponders his powerlessness in an amused, self-communing way. Contrasting the poet's private thoughts and the expressed public voice of the speaker, the suggestion is that there will be time enough for the poet:

> Ah, well, let the sun shine on you
> as it does on a brass plate,
> as it does on a frog's throat,
> as it did on Demosthenes.[48]

The "brass plate" carries simultaneously connotations of status and inferiority: a brass nameplate announces position or authority, and yet it is brass, not gold. In a similar way, "frog's throat" carries the weight of the classical motif of bullfrog as orator and demagogue, but cannot exclude the more everyday inconsequential image. The ambivalence contained in these images is locked into the verse even tighter by the change in the last line to the past tense, positing today against a yesterday and a now-silenced Demosthenes.

The public voice is reported in the local press because it speaks the "right" language of euphemism and sycophancy:

> To speak the truth is more than bad taste.
> It is a treachery to the provost,
> to the bronze-winged angel with the lead shield.[49]

Elders and provosts, church and council, citizen and burgher are all involved in the preservation of a *status quo* which demands pretence and lies, the evasion of truth:

> With every word you now orate
> perpetuate the houses of our fathers
> built of lies, deceit, and sunny weathers
> that hide the sooty rafters of our hate.[50]

The rhyme scheme itself enacts the pattern of truth and evasion: the first and last line above are strong masculine rhymes, "orate" and "hate." There is nothing euphemistic about that second word, either. These are the truths of the poet, and they contain and control the two middle lines which display the weaker feminine rhyme (and two rather clever "ers").

And what is the significance of the poet in this community? A poet has no power, he cannot maintain control through reward or punishment. The poet expands on this powerlessness, slyly contrasting "metaphysical bells" with their "public phone" to admit that poets

> stutter awkwardly when asked to speak
> and when they speak they lose their audience.
> Masters of words, they have no resonance.
> Where you are simple, often they're oblique.[51]

Yet simplicity is condemnation because the "function of Language is not to inform but to evoke."[52] But suddenly, as if grown tired of his small victories over their language, the poet moves from a position within the community, from "you" to "me" and from "we" to "I." With "But let me tell you" he takes up the cliché "they walk on clouds" and breathes life into it:

> The worst of dangers travel from the sky
> as plagues and rockets, planes and birds of prey.

> And, cruising here, drawing my life from clouds,
> I watch such gestures as a clown might make
> arrayed in time and skin like an old sack,
> shapeless below the venom of such birds
> as I am member of.[53]

The reader too experiences a sense of relief as the poet finds his power, his authority, his confidence. "Arrayed in time and skin" is Crichton Smith at his best, arresting, challenging, inspiring. The voice of the poet, as opposed to the civic voice, is oblique and complex. Liberating a tired cliché, he regains territory. Raman Selden describes Barthes' "virtuous writer" as one who "recognises the artifice of all writing and proceeds to make play with it."[54] To make play with writing is to deny an authoritarian insistence on one meaning, and to split asunder the sober partnership of signifier and signified, insisting instead on a rebellious, free-wheeling and uncommitted relationship. The church, the press, the civic leaders in Bourgeois Land authorise meaning. Their power to restrict and limit meaning thus rewrites the Bible as an economic discourse, reduces the ambivalence and ambiguity of the story of Dido and Aeneas to the level of popular romance, appropriates Burns within the discourse of *The Sunday Post*. It is against this authorised "Scottishness" that the poet rebels, positing against one meaning a promiscuous and uncommitted discourse.

In private, too, language is authorised. Language rules rewrite our experiences, hide unpleasant truths. "Farewell Party" is a monologue, the ellipses quoted below pointing up that much is left unexpressed because it need not be expressed. The speaker employs a shared language, a shared joke which operates like traffic lights and whose familiarity makes it understood even in a kind of shorthand communication:

> Oh, it was such a party. Miss MacMillan
> was sitting on the floor in stockinged feet.
> The sherry brimmed and as for the red port . . . !
> Wouldn't have missed it for a hundred million.[55]

Mr Reilly tells jokes about his time in the war, jokes which unlock an experience and make it communicable, in however distorted a form. In the fourth stanza, the public speech does dip towards truth, beginning with the acknowledgement of what lies behind those jokes about the war, and in the gap between "forget" and "anyway":

> Of course he was in the War. He can't forget.
> Anyway it was midnight when we parted.
> I felt so lonely and so broken-hearted.
> I wish the party had been going yet.[56]

"Anyway" gathers up any movement towards felt expression, and although "lonely" and "broken-hearted" appear to express private feeling, "lonely" is subverted by the hyperbolic cliché of "broken-hearted," and any remaining impression of real expressed emotion is swept away by the fact that, against this pain, the party is seen as a suitable analgesic. The poem is a vignette of a public discourse and reveals how the person constructs not just a face to meet other faces, but his or her own identity which imprisons. The cliché with which the poem ends, "That's what I always say," offers a Beckettian mode of survival: repetition as routine. The poem, as a comment on language, is interesting enough. But it lacks the quality of "Retiral."

"Retiral" foregrounds what that public front ignores—the misery of a man released into the "world of Time" who "fights the staring second" by creating a routine. The redundant self inhabits "ghostly earth," a plane much nearer death. But

> Let no one speak of this but still pretend
> it's a beginning when it's just an end
>
> as skeletons make music in the wind
> and crack these dreadful jokes that break the mind.[57]

The "jokes" here are the clichés in which we are inscribed, which deny the truth of our individual experience. Like Eichmann's language rules, they keep the system going smoothly. Crichton Smith offers comment, but the poem stands not because of what is said, but how it is said: "as skeletons make music in the wind" is simply a fine line.

And yet obsessively, Crichton Smith's interest in this volume seems to centre less on metrical experimentation and the creation of sparkling imagery and more on the cracking open of language codes. It is an explorative, perhaps even necessary, volume: Edwin Morgan, in a contemporary review, remarked astutely that the volume represented a step to the side rather than an advance.[58] I believe that Crichton Smith's poetry is all of a piece: a process of exploration where the volumes are all pieces of a larger pattern, discovered and uncovered in the writing. *From Bourgeois Land*, therefore, represents a necessary exploration, the groundwork, for future writing.

Exploring the way language constructs the individual, Crichton Smith's interest extends to popular literature and especially towards magazines aimed at women. In the classroom discussion about Aeneas in *The Last Summer*, one of the students, Miriam, is described by the author as being "bred on Annie S. Swan. The squire leaves the girl in the lurch even though she's a queen."[59] Annie S. Swan is a kind of early Barbara Cartland who wrote romances, short stories and poetry for the popular press. Miriam interprets the tragedy in a simplistic way because she is a product of her society, constructed in and by the kind of literature she reads, the language she is offered. The hero of *My Last Duchess*, Mark Simmons, and his wife are each very much seen as constructed by their reading:

> Her liking for Christmas seemed to him to be on a par with her reading of *Woman's Own* with every appearance of pleasure which to his *New Statesman* mind (slightly stained by the *Spectator*) was like coming across a Wasp in his living room.[60]

And in the title poem from *In The Middle*, the poet observes the patients in a crowded surgery, "reading magazines, their heads bowed. / They turn to the horoscopes and the love stories."[61] Mark Simmons is an intellectual and his wife a housewife. The patients who wait read horoscopes. Crichton Smith's point is that we are constructs of language, "hailed" or called into position as we read. Popular literature, such as that read by Miriam, Mark Simmons's wife, and the patients in the surgery, is written in the tradition of classic realism which Louis Althusser has identified as still dominant and coinciding with the epoch of industrial capitalism.[62] Classic realism insists that language is transparent, denying "the role of language in the construction of the subject."[63] The patients who read horoscopes are encouraged to believe in the fixed identity of the individual: as Catherine Belsey observes astrology insists that identity is fixed, that we cannot change.[64] In the same way, then, "Scottishness" is an ideology created in the language we, as Scots, are given to describe our experience. Tartanry, Kailyardism, far from being peripheral, is as Ian Campbell suggests, inscribed in our language.

The poet has taken up the language of Bourgeois Land, reworked it and found multiple meanings. The discourse of the civic voice can be undermined by the poet, and he can break the "language rule," but "meaning (communication) implies community."[65] Crichton Smith has admitted, "There was a period . . . when I felt . . . a kind of blackness . . . that you are shouting into a room which echoes back to you. . . . It's a hollow echo, there's nothing there."[66] Adopting the persona of Hamlet, the poet has been able to find identity within a community, while remaining outside it. Yet he finds himself in an empty theatre. The "Hamlet" poems in *From Bourgeois Land* and *Hamlet in Autumn* reveal the movement from the positive figure of the spy who keeps his distance to the spy who is excluded. This movement can be illuminated by reference to the second poem in *From Bourgeois Land*, "Entering your house, I sniff again / the Free Church air." In this poem, the poet constructs two circles in order to show his freedom from both. The "I" of the poem is oppressed by the "Free Church" air of the house he enters, an oppression lifted when he walks out into "a bright garden of freer air." "Freer" echoes the "Free" in "Free Church"—echoes, mocks and dismisses it. The poet's oppositions here are the repressive ideology of his religious background and its pre-lapsarian antithesis. This movement turns on the image of a portrait of a young girl, a symbol perhaps of Romantic freedom:

> in an oval frame an eighteen-year-old girl
> like Emily Brontë staring from the peril
> of commandments breaking round her.[67]

The "oval" frame of Romanticism was the circle drawn round the poet, too, which protected him from the "peril of commandments." Against Law, he set Grace. The play on "breaking" above allows the frame to become an island protected against "commandments" yet also acts on these commandments to break them. The "freer air" into which he walks suggests an absence of boundary. The poet looks at the picture, and sees in it an image of freedom, but also an image which defines and confines. He rejects both the Free Church and a Romantic "madness": the mirror of his culture, and the mirror of his earlier poems.

In the Hamlet poems Crichton Smith discovers that the obverse of the freedom of being outwith the frame is exclusion. The identity of Shakespeare's Hamlet is fragmented. He is offered many roles: avenger, son, lover, friend, poet, courtier, madman. Framed on the stage, "a public tragedy," Crichton Smith's Hamlet "saw instead of wigs the curling wreath."[68] Recognising and rejecting the frame, the circle that confines and offers a fixed but false identity, Hamlet exposes his community of actors. Trapped in the role scripted for him, he nevertheless lays bare the artifice of each role. Crichton Smith's Hamlet is a double-edged figure: he is tragic hero and actor, poet and poseur, a reminder, finally, of mortality:

> The machine, powered by history, clicks
> shut like a filing cabinet and on it
> you read Finis not Tragedy.[69]

Crichton Smith's choice of Hamlet as an identity is therefore fruitful. His Hamlet has no stage, no community in which to find an identity reflected back to him. In Bourgeois Land, the public voice, speaking from the civic stage, leaves him dumb:

> It was the flat-faced men with silver borders
> of gold and silver made you live in fire.
>
> It was their speeches robbed you of your speech
> and caused pure silence to reflect your love.[70]

Crichton Smith's Hamlet is offered a fragmented identity. In "Hamlet," the image of the mirror reveals only disharmony:

> Sick of the place, he turned him towards night.
> The mirrors flashed distorted images
> of himself in court dress, with big bulbous eyes,
> and curtains swaying in a greenish light.[71]

Crichton Smith's comment on identity goes some way towards explaining the image above:

> When one is in harmony with the community then one's
> identity is reflected back from the others by a plain mirror and
> not by the exaggerating or attenuating mirrors that one sees in
> fairs.[72]

The poem ends with images which combine the stage metaphor with the image of "air": "imprisoned in this air in which they perish / where only lies and ponderous jokes can flourish."[73] For Crichton Smith the poet, to be born in Scotland was to be born in the wrong place at the wrong time—cast in the wrong part in the wrong play. Calvinist Lewis was seen as hostile: images of TB, and suffocation, perhaps even the growing boy's chronic asthma, revealed Lewis as a place where he could not survive. Bourgeois Land, too, is an alien place where "only lies and ponderous jokes can flourish." Turning from the place and the time in which he was born, the poet has created his own identity. But there is a strong sense that the mirror of his poems is no longer enough: he is excluded from the stage on which the others act— excluded and silenced. "Remove the mirror, for there is no breath," leaves the poet without any identity.

In *From Bourgeois Land*, the poet inhabits a community where language is narrowed and confined and where imagination is limited by the restrictions on language. Using the persona of spy he finds a way of using the clash between individual and community, between the "fine mind" of the poet and a society which seeks to overpower, to annihilate the "secret" of the individual. His oppositions of the Kailyard and "excellence" are personified by an Eichmann figure and by Hamlet. In the last poem in *From Bourgeois Land*, the "disordered man" as Hamlet warns of the Eichmann figure: "Avoid the Man with the Book, the Speech Machine, / and the Rinsoed Boy who is forever clean."[74] "The" book, with its definite article, the "Speech Machine," a standardised, automatic language, posits power as language, a power which reduces the importance of the individual. The "Rinsoed Boy" is "forever clean" because his language will have no individual resonance: his ability to describe and recognise his own unique experience and carry it with him will be negated.

Although this volume contains only a few of the poems which can be ranked among Crichton Smith's best, there is no doubt that the identity of a Hamlet figure has been fruitful. It has allowed him to establish an identity within a community yet to remain apart from it. Much of the problem with the poetry comes from relinquishing too much—from a sense of being overpowered by the mediocre and the mundane. Yet on the imaginative level, Crichton Smith has begun to expose the identity created in his own poems as a "pose," a role. "Hamlet always talks of death" because "he saw it clear."[75] Role playing, the poet makes the discovery on the imaginative level that his own creation is flawed: like Hamlet's fellow actors, the identities created in his poems ignore mortality. On the imaginative level, the stage set of his poems begins to be revealed, his role of actor is foregrounded. But it is the death of Crichton Smith's mother, Christina, which catapults the poet towards a rigorous and terrible examination of the mirror of his poetry: to the abandonment of what comes to be seen as "shabby skins" and towards a barer, harder language, honed not through language games on an intellectual level but by the intrusion into that game of the physical world.

Notes

1. Ian Campbell, *Kailyard: A New Assessment* (Edinburgh: Ramsay Head, 1981), pp. 10-11.
2. *Ibid.*, p. 8.
3. *Ibid.*, p. 16.
4. John McQueen, *Lines Review* 29 (June 1969), 46-48 (p. 47).
5. *Seven Poets* (Glasgow: Third Eye, 1981), p. 47.
6. *Thistles and Roses* (London: Eyre & Spottiswoode, 1961), p. 15.
7. "Scotland: The Facts For All To See," *Scottish Review* (Autumn 1976), 3-7 (p. 4; p. 3).
8. *The Law and the Grace* (London: Eyre & Spottiswoode, 1965), p. 58.
9. *The Arden Shakespeare: King Lear*, edited by Kenneth Muir (London: Methuen, 1964), V 3 17.
10. Josiah Thompson, *The Lonely Labyrinth: Kierkegaard's Pseudonymous Works* (Carbondale: Illinois University Press, 1967), p. 34.
11. Interview with Iain Crichton Smith, Taynuilt, 1987.
12. *Thistles and Roses*, p. 35.
13. *New Poets*, edited by Edwin Muir (London: Eyre & Spottiswoode, 1959), p. 25.
14. Private Correspondence, 4 March 1988.
15. Review of "The MacDiarmids. A Conversation—Hugh MacDiarmid and Duncan Glen," *Akros*, 6:16 (April 1971), 57-58 (p. 57).
16. Lorn Macintyre, "Poet in Bourgeois Land," *Scottish International* (September 1971), 22-27 (p. 26).
17. Review of "The MacDiarmids. A Conversation—Hugh MacDiarmid and Duncan Glen," p. 57.
18. *Penguin Modern Poets 21* (London: Penguin, 1972), p. 78.
19. *Seven Poets*, p. 44.
20. Penguin Modern Poets, p. 67.

21. "Between Sea and Moor," in *As I Remember*, edited by Maurice Lindsay (London: Hale, 1979), pp. 107-121 (p. 115).
22. *Penguin Modern Poets 21*, p. 72.
23. "Scotch and Wry," BBC Television, December 31, 1987.
24. *Penguin Modern Poets 21*, p. 72.
25. "Poet in Bourgeois Land," pp. 25-26.
26. *Penguin Modern Poets 21*, p. 79.
27. *From Bourgeois Land* (London: Gollancz, 1969), p. 10.
28. Hannah Arendt, *Eichmann In Jerusalem* (London: Penguin, 1979), pp. 287-288.
29. *Lines Review* 29 (June 1969), 46-48 (p. 47).
30. R. H. Tawney, *Religion And The Rise Of Capitalism: A Historical Survey* (London: Murray, 1933).
31. Adorno, T. W., Else Frenkel-Brunswick, Daniel J. Levinson, R. Nevitt Sandford, *The Authoritarian Personality* (New York: Norton, 1965).
32. Erich Fromm, *The Fear Of Freedom* (London: Routledge, 1966), pp. 95-96.
33. Catherine Belsey, *Cricital Practice* (London: Methuen, 1980), p. 5.
34. *The Law and the Grace*, p. 38.
35. *From Bourgeois Land*, p. 20.
36. *Ibid.*
37. *Ibid.*, pp. 31-32.
38. *Ibid.*, p. 32.
39. *Ibid.*, p. 38.
40. *Ibid.*, p. 39.
41. *Ibid.*
42. *Ibid.*, p. 16.
43. *The Last Summer* (Glasgow: Drew, 1986), pp. 99-100.
44. "Poet in Bourgeois Land," p. 26.
45. *West Highland Free Press*, 6 June 1986, p. 3. Reprinted in *The End of A Régime* edited by Brian Filling and Susan Stuart (Aberdeen: University Press, 1991), p. 123.
46. *Ibid.*, 23 May 1986, p. 1.
47. Taynuilt Interview.
48. *From Bourgeois Land*, p. 13.
49. *Ibid.*
50. *Ibid.*
51. *Ibid.*, p. 15.
52. Anthony Wilden, *The Language of the Self* (Baltimore: Johns Hopkins University Press, 1968), pp. 62-63.
53. *From Bourgeois Land*, p. 15.
54. Raman Selden, *A Reader's Guide to Contemporary Literary Theory* (London: Harvester, 1985), p. 74.
55. *From Bourgeois Land*, p. 30.
56. *Ibid.*
57. *Ibid.*, p. 52.
58. Edwin Morgan, *Scottish International* (November 1969), p. 61.
59. *The Last Summer*, p. 99.
60. *My Last Duchess* (London: Gollancz, 1972), p. 33.
61. *In The Middle* (London: Gollancz, 1977), p. 9.
62. *Critical Practice*, p. 67.
63. *Ibid.*
64. *Ibid.*, p. 64.
65. Tzevetan Todorov, *Mikhail Bakhtin: The Dialogical Principle*, translated by Wlad Godzich (Manchester: Manchester University Press, 1984), p. 30.

66. *Seven Poets*, p. 47.
67. *From Bourgeois Land*, p. 11.
68. "Carol and Hamlet," *Hamlet in Autumn* (Edinburgh: Macdonald, 1972), p. 13; p. 14.
69. "Finis not Tragedy," *Hamlet in Autumn*, p. 59.
70. *From Bourgeois Land*, p. 25.
71. *Ibid.*, p. 18.
72. "Real People in a Real Place," in *Towards the Human* (Edinburgh: Macdonald, 1986), p. 24.
73. *From Bourgeois Land*, p. 18.
74. *Ibid.*, p. 61.
75. *Hamlet in Autumn*, p. 14.

III
Outcast

CHAPTER FOUR

Orpheus

"Everything I have ever done is really eventually coming to this question. What is death? What is a dead person, and in the end what is the value of writing when one is confronted by a dead person?"[1] Crichton Smith's comment in 1971 suggests that the poet has become aware of the conflict he has been exploring on the imaginative level: the old woman, the carcass of the sheep, have always confronted the poet with the death's head. But the breakthrough into the perilous zone is occasioned by a sudden shift in perspective. The experience of the writer here, suddenly become reader of his own work, is the experience of the viewer of Holbein's *The Ambassadors*. Holbein offers the viewer a study of two finely-robed sons of the Renaissance surrounded by symbols of their culture. Towards the front of the picture plane is a distorted image. It is only as the eye retreats from the painting that the image is recognised: it is a skull. What appears first as a painting of two proud figures straddling the sum of human knowledge suddenly transforms itself into the coat of arms of death. The broken lute string, the skull, these clues have been there all along but have been misrecognised till now. The picture reveals perspective as a certain stance.[2] Crichton Smith's poetry has always contained within its canvas too the death's head, but it is only with a sudden shift in perspective that it is recognised by the poet. Crichton Smith's mother, Christina, died in 1969. It is that event which decentres the perspective of the poet and allows him to enter into a perilous zone where looking back he recognises the death's head. The personae of the diamond-browed one, of Hamlet, like Holbein's Ambassadors, are exposed as actors, poseurs.

Up to this point in his career, Crichton Smith has been forging an identity, creating his philosophy. The death of his mother plunges him into a ruthless examination of his creation and to the destruction of the frame which separates life and art. Crichton Smith's comment in 1987 about his mental breakdown shows a sudden illumination of the discoveries of his poetry: "I wondered . . . if someone creates a major theory, whether as I was doing he leaves out the things that don't fit in and just puts in the things that fit. . . . I was just picking out the bits of all the flux to fit in with my own ideas."[3] The comment reveals perspective as point of view, and a growing suspicion that it is fragmentary and perhaps even dishonest. The death of his mother therefore is an event which changes not just the poetry of the 1972 volume *Love Poems and Elegies* but marks a watershed in the poet's work, reverberating throughout the subsequent volumes.

I have shown how in earlier poems the death's head makes the poet stutter because his instinct to transcend through art is tethered by recognition of the physical fact of death. Exploration of this conflict is exploration of point of view. For example, Crichton Smith's treatment of the *Iolaire* disaster is very different from contemporary poems, not just because it does not offer a personal response to the disaster but because it refuses the consolations of Calvinism. I have already shown how the disaster affected the poet and his community. Certainly it would seem to demand a response in art from a poet with his background. Crichton Smith was drawn to the subject matter: "I spent many years thinking I should write something about this. And I did. But I wasn't satisfied with it."[4] In fact, Crichton Smith wrote three poems on the tragedy; "The Iolaire," "After The War," and "Iolaire." The first two are separated from the third not just by the years between their publication but by the difference in the poet's response: the third poem was written by a man who had experienced his mother's death.

The first poem was published in *Saltire Review* in 1957 and tells of the tragedy through the words of a sailor eventually rescued. The source of Crichton Smith's subsequent dissatisfaction with the poem might best be illuminated by comparison with Lowell's "A Quaker Graveyard in Nantucket." Here, the Italian *canzone* is adapted in a way suggestive of "Lycidas." At the beginning of his poem, Lowell offers the inscription:

> Let man have dominion over the fishes of the sea and the fowls of the air and the beasts and the whole earth and every creeping creature that moveth upon the earth.[5]

Patrick Cosgrave makes the point that what Lowell's poem shows is that men do not have dominion.[6] Recasting these fishes, fowls, sea, earth, air, and beasts in the context of myth, he shifts perspective and allows Poseidon, the consort of earth and Lord of Earthquake, the dominating role. In a similar way, Crichton Smith inscribes the *Iolaire* disaster in a mythical text: his God is not the God of Calvinism, but a dehumanised God, perhaps even Lowell's Poseidon:

Shark-headed God snaps from his gardened calm.
His teeth bite cleanly and the fragrance burns
heavy with fruit and salt.
        The void mouth yearns![7]

Crichton Smith refuses to allow Calvinism to redeem here, to redeem
the irredeemable, but slides into a sensuous celebration of tragedy. Art
redeems. The tragedy seen by Lewis people as domestic and personal,
a tragedy redeemed by their Calvinist religion, has been overwhelmed
by an image which encompasses a monster and the arbitrariness of
Poseidon. Shifting perspective, he transposes the tragedy on to a canvas
of Greek mythology. Art as redemption later becomes suspect. Yet the
poem is important because it usefully reveals the way in which
Crichton Smith's response differs from other poems written on the
subject.

Traditionally, it has been thought that it is through art that we can
order and transcend experience, neaten the ragged edges. This impulse
is clear in other poems which were written at the time of the disaster.
Shortly after the disaster, a benefit was held by the Highland Societies
in Glasgow in the King's Theatre. A "Prologue Spoken by the
Players" was specially written by Neil Munro and delivered by a
famous Shakespearian actor of the time, Sir John Martin Harvey. The
perspective here is that of Sophoclean Tragedy. The island, accustomed
to tragedy, accepts its history of loss; men die in wars and on the
terrible seas. The poem transcends the casual nature of the event simply
through performance: it dignifies and orders. The actual content of the
poem also transcends the casual by suggesting that it is part of a larger
unseen pattern. The foundering of the *Iolaire* is another part of the
island's history, an island "destined to tears."[8] A contemporary poem
by John N. Maciver, "Home at Last," takes refuge in the idea of death
as a final homecoming:

So near their home, and yet so far that never, never more
They'll roam the dreaming moorland, or by the lone sea-shore.
Theirs be the calm of heaven, the peace the world denied
After life's cruel tempest, the hush of eventide.
Home at last![9]

Many Gaelic poems were written too but surprisingly more enduring
was a ballad in English which was taken up by the children and which
kept alive for them a disaster they were too young to remember. It too
ends with the idea of a heavenly homecoming after life's tempestuous
seas:

            Their storms in life are over
            Their anchors safely cast

79

> In that celestial harbour
> With God himself at last.[10]

All these poems evade the accidental by perceiving in it a larger plan. The last two specifically perceive it as the journey of these men from an imperfect, real world, to the ideal of a heaven.

Crichton Smith's poem substitutes a Greek God for the God of Calvinism, and can therefore seize on the essential tragedy. It is the idea of catastrophe, the irrational nature of the tragedy, which focuses the second poem, "After The War." "They plunged to nonsense" and "clutching nothing in absurd fist," refuse the consolations of Calvinism, but here the poet side-steps redemption through art and becomes the poet of Bourgeois Land, the outsider who inspects justice through a queer air:

> And I who would most dearly play my best
> aspiring bugle-tune, while sea consumes,
> mile upon mile, the foolish and the wise,
> find little here to praise
> except the knowledge that these varying tombs
> remind absurdity of our interest.[11]

Denial of that bugle-tune, however, gives it utterance.

Discussing "The Iolaire," a critic in the *Stornoway Gazette* suggested the poem "lacks something of the emotional intensity of those written under the immediate impact of the disaster, but from the literary stand-point it is in a class by itself."[12] The "literary stand-point," the point of view which precludes other perspectives, is what Crichton Smith begins to question. It is significant that his third poem about the disaster, "Iolaire," shows a movement towards psychological involvement. He explains

> I imagine an elder of the Free Church standing on the shore watching all this happening, because what really bothered me was the question, What did this event do to such people's faith? In fact I know nothing about this, I have never read or seen that it did anything.[13]

"Iolaire," like the poet's earlier poems on the disaster, does not attempt to impose a pattern on the events but rather explores and perhaps even celebrates the accidental, casual nature of catastrophe:

> in sloppy waves,
> in the fat of water, they came floating home
> bruising against their island. It is true,
> a minor error can inflict this death.[14]

The poem ends not with the "dry and prayerless prayers" of the 1959 poem but with imagery of water, baptism and rebirth into the freedom of Godlessness:

> This water soaks me. I am running with
> its tart sharp joy. I am floating here
> in my black uniform. I am embraced
> by these green ignorant waters. I am calm.[15]

The tragedy is not inscribed in terms of Greek tragedy nor Highland Calvinism: the poet's focus is on inner experience and an ambiguous liberation.

Crichton Smith's question about the *Iolaire* disaster was "what did this event do to people's faith?" The death of his mother in 1969 meant that this question is one he had to answer himself, and though the faith challenged is not a religious faith, it is the faith that makes sense of his own universe and his belief in his art. The silent judge of his poetry has always been the old woman in black of his islands. In *Love Poems and Elegies* the interlocutor becomes more particularly his mother and what she represents of the Calvinistic inheritance.

What kind of woman was Christina Campbell? Born on the island of Lewis, she became a fisher girl, following the herring fleets, gutting the huge barrels of fish on the windswept quays of Lowestoft and Stornoway in cold dawns. Her marriage to John Smith produced three sons, and the youngest of them was just a baby when her husband died of TB while they were living in Glasgow because of John's work as a Merchant Seaman. After his death she returned to Lewis to raise the three boys on around a pound a week widow's pension. Even by Lewis standards, they were poor. That poverty has left its mark on the poet: tramps haunt his work, and he admits that during the terrible black months of his mental breakdown, it was the fear of poverty that tormented him. Yet there was still dignity, still a sense of tradition. "We used to have salt herring and potatoes every day of the week, except on Sunday. On Sunday we always had meat." Sundays were for church-going, too:

> My mother was a very religious woman. She belonged to the Free
> Church and I remember . . . she used to talk about the ministers that
> they used to have up in Lewis and she used to rate them almost like
> film stars and they would say oh this man was a wooden minister—
> this is a Gaelic expression—this meant that they had no actual
> passion, that probably they read the sermon from notes and what
> they were looking for was someone who was really passionate and
> made them think that they were going to hell the following day.

The progression from "she" to "these women" seems to group his mother with the "old women" of his island. Christina Campbell seems to have been a woman very much at home in the culture of the island. If Crichton Smith has said "she had a very strong character" he has

F

written little directly about her. What is certain is that he rejected much that was offered to him of the Lewis culture. To be the son of a woman who embodies that culture reveals a deep and central conflict. His mother is admired and feared, loved and hated. A similar slide from "them" to "my mother" in the following comment suggests strongly that the conflicts in the poetry reflect the conflicts in his relationship with his mother:

> On the one side I don't like them in a certain way because of a self-righteousness but on the other hand I always admire their strength because they're always willing to come out and say what they think and they've got this extraordinary willpower and strength which I think my mother had. In many ways she was a remarkable woman. And bringing up three boys on eighteen shillings a week was no joke.[16]

Crichton Smith's comment on Mrs Scott in *Consider the Lilies* is an attempt to deny a sentimental reading of the character: "she seems to me like some of the Highland women I have known. She has a strong unbreakable will and is oppposed to life in some ways."[17] It reveals an ambivalent response of admiration and dislike. The relationship between Malcolm and his mother in *The Last Summer* suggests a young boy straining to develop his individuality where community is all-important, and becoming secretive and defensive. The novel is loosely based on Crichton Smith's own experience and may reveal much about his relationship with his mother. More particularly, he describes his own feelings of alienation in an autobiographical memoir:

> I would return at night from the school and do my homework—I remember mainly geometry problems and Latin—by the light of the Tilley lamp on the oil-clothed table, and felt more and more a gap opening between me on the one side and my mother and brother on the other side. So I withdrew into myself and never discussed anything that had happened in the school as if it were a secret world which I treasured and didn't want tampered with at any cost.[18]

The gap which opens between mother and son, between history and self, between Calvinist Lewis and a private world, is one which the poet has already begun to explore by the time of his mother's death. But the event catastrophically ruptures connection completely. The poet who has abandoned his community suddenly discovers a terrible freedom.

The gap is terrifying yet liberating. The poems which "sprang directly from the death of my mother" show two distinct movements: a desire to write across that gap, and an impulse which appears to crush a creative response. Negotiating these conflicts, the poet discovers a harder, barer verse.

The poems which reveal a desire to write across the gap nevertheless acknowledge the discoveries of "For My Mother": mother and son inhabit different worlds. At seventeen, Crichton Smith embarked on student life in Aberdeen. At seventeen, his mother was a fisher-girl, following the fleet:

> You on the other hand were gutting herring
> (at seventeen) on a hard Lowestoft quay
> with glassy hands to which dark blood would cling
> while the red clouds would lighten on the sea.
>
> Angrily I watch you from my guilt
> and sometimes think: The herring in my hand,
> bloody and gutted, would be far more solid
> than this more slippery verse.[19]

The conversational "You on the other hand" sets up the poet's concern here with comparison, and with the differences between mother and son. One hand and the other hand may seem familiar but they are different. "Hand" which begins its life as a cliché takes on new life almost immediately by its proximity to the manual task of "gutting herring." "Glassy hands" become "my hand." "Gutting" becomes "gutted." The "dark blood" which clings to the hand is reflected by, but is different from, the "red clouds" which "lighten on the sea." The poem turns on repetitions and reflections, uncovering the differences. The gap can never be bridged.

The double movements of comparison with difference, of admiration and anger, of the mother figure seen as both the source, and the denial, of his art, are constantly worked through in *Love Poems and Elegies* in poems which seek to write across the gap. In the opening poem, the rhythm of nursery rhyme ghosts the more formal rhythm:

> my constant aim
> to find a ghost within a close who speaks
> in Highland Gaelic.[20]

The assonance in the middle line above suggests a hollow echo. He discovers "I do not find your breath in the air." The line reads lightly, but the volume's vocabulary constantly turns on the ideas of breath, air and suffocation, so that contained within the line is the suggestion that the search for evidence of his mother's life, her history, and therefore his history, is a lifeline, a way to bridge the gap that declares him outcast. Yet nothing remains of her here. There are memorials to the dead heroes of the war: "Everywhere there are statues. Stone remains. / The mottled flesh is transient."[21]

The Glasgow the poet wanders in now is not the Glasgow his

mother knew, a Glasgow of markets and flat-caps and music hall. He can recreate that only through her memories, a second-hand knowledge, and in many ways a reductive stereotype. The line, "'There was such warmth,' you said . . ." pulls the poem in two different directions revealing the tensions here. The quotation marks both bring his mother into the poem by giving her speech and yet also lock her out of his poem by physically separating her speech from his. The use of the past tense within the immediacy of the poet's discourse also reveals disjunction. The poem of tribute explores separation, the gap between two people. "The past's an experience we cannot share" accepts that each has had a different history which has shaped and moulded and therefore separated. As he did in "Aberdeen," the poet uses comparisons to reveal differences. Standing in Glasgow

> I stand in a cleaner city, better fed,
> in my diced coat, brown hat, my paler hands
> leafing a copy of the latest book.[22]

The comparatives "cleaner," "better," "paler" unite and yet separate and culminate in the superlative, "latest." Is this the poet's own book? Whether it is or not, the book acts as a metaphor for the poet's education, a process that drew him from his background, for the English texts in which he chose to find an identity, and for the world of poetry which has provided a "world beyond this world." Absorbed into this poem is the imagery of the earlier poem "Aberdeen": "paler hands" and "leafing a copy of the latest book" have their counterpart in the red chapped hands gutting herring, and the hand which writes slippery verse.

"Leafing a copy of the latest book" offers a casual reader. The motif of reader is important in the poems about his mother and "casual" in turn reflects on an obsessive need now to read his mother's life. He reads his mother's life through what she tells him, in a photograph of fisher girls, in the religion of his island. The position of reader is not "casual" but nevertheless insists on distance and describes his isolation. Looking at a photograph of a group of young girls taken at the fishing, the poet sees not just the central group, but the frame and beyond the frame:

> In that brown picture you all look very old
> for twenty-year-old girls and you're all gazing
> to a sun that's off the edge and is made of salt.[23]

These lives are contained and constrained, framed not just by the edge of the photograph but by their world. Lips do not smile, and the sun is salt.

The frame in "That Island Formed You" is the island itself; an island

84

of "black hatted men / and stony bibles." And if the young fisher girls
could gaze towards a sun off the edge with the optimism of youth, here
"the heart's devoured / by the black rays of a descending sun."[24] The
poet recognises the frame which constricts, recognises too how lives are
self-limited: "Always they're making fences, making barred / gates to
keep the wind out."[25] The island life is harsh, its religion severe.
Excluded from the frame is grace: the poet brings into the poem earlier
images of daffodil, and a life-giving, unbounded "waste abundant air."
These are no longer set in opposition to law, to the Calvinist culture,
but are claimed by the poet—and by his mother. "They're" and
"these" set the people of the island forever apart from his mother as
she is reclaimed "my dear" to share his joys.

"You told me once" recounts what his mother has told him of her
own brother's death by drowning when he was swept off a trawler and
of his singing a psalm in the hope of attracting rescue. His own
mother's death is described as a reflection of that death: the image in
both is suffocation, and the pronoun "you" marks not just a change
of subject but links together "you" and "he" and the relationship
"your brother":

> You died of lack of oxygen. I tried
> to fit the mask against your restless face
> in the bumpy ambulance in which you lay.[26]

The images of oxygen and of mask surface again in "The Space Ship."
Working with comparison, the poet looks at a picture, a copy of
reality:

> I think of you and then I think of this
> picture of an astronaut lacking air,
> dying of lack of it in the depths of space.[27]

Enacted in the lines is the circularity of the poet's thoughts, centring
on his mother, and her death. The poem ends with the image of a
helmet fitting over the face. It is an image of suffocation and perhaps
death, but inscribed in a text of epiphany:

> The black mediaeval helmet fits his face
> and the glass breaks without a single sound
> and becomes the crystals of unnumbered stars.[28]

The images of oxygen, suffocation and helmets are rooted in Crichton
Smith's background: his chronic asthma and the ever-present fear of
TB, the war and the necessity of gas masks which he found difficult to
manage. They appear throughout his work, but with more intensity
in *Love Poems and Elegies*.

In conflict with the movement to write across the gap are poems which impose limitations on the creative response. As if in direct response to his question, "What is the point of writing when one is confronted by a dead person?", the poet in "On looking at the dead" writes

> This is a coming to reality.
> This is the stubborn place. No metaphors swarm
>
> around that fact, around that strangest thing,
> that being that was and now no longer is.[29]

The poet of *The Long River* who created powerful metaphors in defiance of a bare background now insists on a bare language, as if there were a language free of metaphor, as if now accepting the Calvinist suspicion of "graven images." Despite "this is," "that fact," "that strangest thing," "that being that was and now no longer is," which attempt such bareness, "no metaphors swarm" is itself a metaphor and gives the lie to the instistence that there is a creative use of language and something purely referential. "It only is itself. / It isn't you. It only is itself" returns to the bareness of labelling "it" and of comparison which is stripped to the basic "is" and "isn't." This harshness is welcomed: it provides a terrible single perspective now for the poet:

> having it as centre, for you take
> directions from it not as from a book
>
> but from this star, black and fixed and here.[30]

The experience of death is valued and celebrated because it is "not as from a book" but real, "therefore central and of major price." Turning from his position of reader of his mother's life, he explores personal response from a dangerously limited perspective.

Wallace Stevens' "Anecdote of the Jar" is seen as "exemplar of the exotic" and rejected for images of the narrowing circle, the bible and blackness:

> if I shall say I had a jar it would
> be a black mountain in the Hebrides
>
> and round it fly your blackbirds black as pitch
> and in their centre with a holy book
>
> a woman all in black reading the world
> consisting of black crows in a black field.[31]

Yet the movement of the narrowing circle, the fixed and limited perspective, is countered by the movement of the poet's thoughts. The conditional "If I shall say I had" and "it would be" pull against the insistent "and" which lists overpowering images of limitation. The insistent "black," used seven times in a poem which, including the title, is just sixty-four words long, is both destructive and creative. It attempts to destroy and almost annihilate the movement towards an imaginative use of language, yet its repetition shows the poet using it in a stylised, creative way which overcomes the power of the word. To compare this poem with poems from *The Long River* is to compare a poet who is searching, raiding the language, with a poet who has evolved a distinctive language, distinctive movements, characteristic imagery and patterning. The deep image of the circle, the colour black, images of suffocation and air, the old woman, these have been the substance of his poetry all along but here he returns to them with an exciting yet dangerous obsession, finding in constraint and limitation a new and disciplined creativity.

The danger lies in embracing this perspective totally. "This clutch of black grapes" brings a Keatsean sensuousness to his verse. This "clutch of black stars" has its own luxuriousness; it is special and only for fine palates:

> their sweetness and their tartness oozing out
> in such a taste as hardly we can bear
> fattened by an ordinary sun,
>
> a sun so white and common in the sky
> which bred this constellation, this swart tribe,
> this galaxy of stars so sweet and black.[32]

"Swart" permits linguistic variation even for blackness here: yet that variation is so self-conscious that "black" is brought back into the line by its obvious evasion. This "clutch of black stars" is Crichton Smith's poetry refined, confined, limited by a new experience. It is an experience not of the isolated artist, in a world beyond this world, testing his language in a theoretical or analytical way, but common to everyone. The subject of the line, "fattened by an ordinary sun," seems to be "we" but the use of "fattened" makes it ambiguously refer to the grapes, too. This "white and common sun" produces the grapes and us as well. The white of the sun and the blackness of the grapes are part of the same process. His experience is not unique. The poet's language here, "sweetness," "tartness," "oozing," "taste," "swart" and "sweet," insists on a sense of taste and a sensuous gratification: "they seem like globes of death but they are sweet, / the gravities and bells of our desire."[33] Not wishing to transcend the experience he is in danger of being locked inside it.

In these poems, Crichton Smith faces the kind of challenge which he has suggested produces the greatest poetry:

I believe that the greatest poetry is created at the moment when you are at the frontiers. That is to say, when you are absorbing and transforming new material.[34]

The new material here that Crichton Smith deals with is not the abstract death's head which ghosts the earlier poetry but the real historical experience of the death of his mother. It is this personal experience that has allowed the poet to discover a flaw in his system. Contemporary poems on the *Iolaire* disaster found comfort in religion, in the belief in an ideal world, a heaven, beyond life. Crichton Smith's solace, too, came from a world beyond this world and the comfort offered was his art. If this art is now suspect, if it has been violated by an event in the historical world, how can he continue? In "Argument," the poet confronts the "Terror of pure nothingness" to ask

> if behind
> the stubborn stone there isn't more than stone
> how shall we find direction?

The Greek religion was based on ideals:

> The Greeks believed the circle was the perfect
> figure. Therefore the heavens must conform.
> There had to be a way to make ellipses
> respectable and so explain the orbit
> of planets moving gravely through the light.
> It just required a little movement of
> a human mind, a justice as of love.[35]

It is seen as a paradigm imposed on a reality organised differently, and ultimately inadequate. "Therefore" and "must conform" insist that everything must be explainable. "There had to be" sounds a little more desperate and "respectable" has an almost pejorative reverberation to it, as if this desire to neaten, to control chaos, is basically a kind of bourgeois weakness.

For the poet, too, there is a desperate need for the ideals of art, for the world beyond this world, and yet his mother's death has forced a new perspective which illuminates the misfit between reality and the paradigm with which he attempts to master it.

As if finding a basis from which to offer an answer of affirmation to the question, "what is the value of writing when one is confronted by a dead person?", the question which confronts him at his mother's death, he writes from "a certain stance." The stance therefore does not deny the "terror of pure nothingness" but allows for something beyond the everyday. There will still be moments of joy:

> O there are moments when a certain star
> rising over the waters is a song,

a glove, a perfume, a remembrancer,
a soul steadily rising.[36]

His stance is "certain" and uncertain, acknowledging the partiality of
such a stance which occludes other stances. A "certain" stance is also
a necessary stance, because now he can overcome the self-imposed
limitations of poems like "This clutch of grapes" where the poet seems
to glut himself on the totality of restriction. A certain stance allows for
that necesssary distance:

> so I know
> that death is just a place that we have looked
> too deeply at, not into, as at a book
> held that short space too close. For we must hold
> back from a painting so as to see it whole.[37]

The personal experience of his mother's death has taken him "too
close." Finally the poet can choose his perspective, and see the whole
canvas, no longer just the death's head. In Holbein's painting, just
behind the curtain, there is a crucifix which invites faith in a divine
knowledge to replace transient, worldly knowledge. The whole
painting reassures that death is not a finality but a transformation. "We
must hold / back from a painting so as to see it whole" delivers the
poet from "I" to "we," from personal to universal, yet his
transformation is less reassuring than Holbein's: "certain stance" and
"hold back" reveal a much more uncomfortable, volatile position.

The poet rejects, too, the transformation from wordly to ideal. In
"The chair in which you've sat," the movement is from the purity of
abstraction towards the human. Touching on Plato's Theory of Ideas,
the poet's sparse language allows each referent another existence as a
pure signifier:

> The chair in which you've sat's not just a chair
> nor the table at which you've eaten just a table
> nor the window that you've looked from just a window.[38]

In Plato's theory, these ultimate referents were the originals situated in
an ideal world, of which the chairs, tables and windows in the human
world were just copies. Here the poet reverses the hegemony of the
model. Ideals are "just" ideals, and put aside for the human:

> and yet more lovely because truly human,
> as tables, chairs and windows in our world
> are ours and loved because they taste of us.
> Being who we are we must adore the common
> copies of perfection, for the grace
> of perfect things and angels is too cold.[39]

"Grace" is an important word in the poet's vocabulary. Its use here is significant as he distances himself from the earlier poet who found grace and perfection in a poetry separated from the ordinary, from the human. The linking of "perfect things and angels" mocks perfection because an angel is a signifier without a referent, an ideal for which there is no human copy. Here is a new tone; human, limited, restricted to the world around him. Yet any feeling of complacency is swiftly dispelled by the image with which the poem ends: "startlingly striking out of the air / the tigerish access of a crumpled glove." There is a double image of space here: the "air" and the "access" of the glove. The glove offers a figure of doubleness, too, in that it is the shape of a hand. A glove's ideal form is the ideal form of the hand. " Crumpled glove" indicates imperfection and yet the normal malleability of things. The image insists that the human does not conform to the pure idea or ideal. "Tigerish," on the one level a simple description of a fur-lined glove, contains within it the menace of the tiger, the real animal and Blake's tiger. Imperfection, malleability, change, are all alien to the world of ideas yet make our human world exciting.

The poet's achievement in the elegies for his mother is to transform material at the frontiers. He has not idealised his mother, or her death, and the general lack of pattern reveals the raggedness of experience: sometimes surmounted for the moment, sometimes confronted again with fresh grief. The last poem underlines this lack of pattern:

> Your marble tombstone stands up like a book.
> The storms have not read it nor the leaves.
> The blue lightnings bounced from it.
> The ignorant swallows perched on its top.[40]

The only pattern is repetition and recircling, a movement encapsulated in "I have forgotten it over and over." The line which seeks comfort in celebrating the human, "Life is explainable only by life," is a neat, symmetrical and satisfying line but "explainable" sprawls across that neatness and it is finally damned by the last line of the sequence, "I have read that on paper leaves." "Paper leaves" points to "leaves" in the second line quoted above forcing the reader to leap over the idea of "paper leaves" as being copies of real leaves and comprehend that these are pages of a book. The comparison between the tombstone unread by storms, lightnings and swallows, and the paper leaves he reads for comfort, is a comparison between an inhuman perfection and a common humanity and compromise, between the ideal and the human.

The poems for his mother are both elegies and love poems. Correspondingly, the love poems in this volume are also elegies. They are produced in the shadow of poems about death, and they relinquish much that is associated with love poetry. In the elegies, the poet refused to adopt an idealised image of death. His love poems, too, insist on taking account of our "limited human existence":

> I believe that a romantic attitude will no longer be sufficient . . . I believe that the sort of love poetry which can profitably be written will be one which takes account of our limited human existence.[41]

Here is the shock of a poet structuring his art on book-keeping terms: "sufficient," "profitably" and "takes account" weighs and judges without passion, opposing romance and the sweeping gesture. More specifically he calls Burns's poetry to judgement:

> Lines of the order of "And I will love thee still, my dear, / Till a' the seas gang dry" will no longer be possible. Their romance is too huge, their hope too expansive. It will be pointless to compare women with roses, for these they are not. It is possible that when women were passive, politically and domestically, they could be regarded as roses. Now we understand that they are inconceivably other. They are seen to be, like ourselves, dying in time, tormented by time, altering us and themselves.[42]

What kind of love poetry can be written after this manifesto? The opening poem in this section, "No-one at home," reveals that the poems of love share the vocabulary of the poems of death:

> I remember
> you standing with a cocktail in your hand.
> You were as white as an eel I saw once,
> upright in the water, almost dead.
> It was an angel of the endless waste.
> You are an angel whose bubbles are all gone.[43]

The poem plays with water imagery, with death by drowning, and the last line quoted above quirkily links up with "cocktail" to provide a sudden image of dead champagne or carbonated drinks. Lost love is a death, too.

In "The dream" the book-keeper-poet can insist "There is no / romance in our natures, only a safe keeping." The ambiguity of "safe keeping" includes the sense of emotion repressed and locked away. These surface in a dream, however, to echo the images of the elegies to his mother and reveal a sense of tragic loss:

> I dream a dream. With a green ring in my hand
> I'm drifting towards you, we are great moon bears
> hulking in light. And then you drift away.
> Hiking my oxygen I follow you.

And then I am alone. The space-ship's gone.
You're at the window, white face peering out.
The taxi streams in rain past a green star.[44]

In "Resurrection" there is a rare note of irony from the poet as he parallels the underworld with "last night's party" and uses the line end to create a gap in "A Venus from the blue / scarred flowing ashtrays." The book-keeper-poet is constantly undermined because his language continually acknowledges its antithesis: the language of romance, of the huge gesture, of the literature of love. "The fever" insists

> In ruinous excess to go out into the night
> was left to Romeo and Juliet.
>
> For our part we burn with a steady fever,
> separate though together, the heat that comes from each
> not quite enough to make the one star.[45]

The positioning and cadence of "ruinous excess" allows this thought to be savoured before the brisk return to "for our part." And "not quite enough to make the one star" surely suggests a longing for MacDiarmid's "Consummation," "Until in crystal heat, O Love Sublime, / One with eternity our bodies glow."[46] The book-keeper-poet admonishes MacDiarmid for his adolescent, mystical passion: the poet mourns the distance between them. In "Love, if you are love" the book-keeper-poet hesitates to identify the emotion and the poem straddles a nervous mixture of romantic discourses, now the "lightly tremble" of Mills and Boon and now the stoical "unsinews" of Elizabethan drama:

> So
> a phone can ring but sometimes it does not.
> The heart may lightly tremble for its ring
> whose harsh sonority unsinews it.[47]

"Can" and "does not" reveal the basic oppositions of the elegies and the same distrust of the sweeping gesture. In the elegies, the desire to write across the gap was held in tension by a distrust of language. In the love poems, the same distrust of language limits the response.

The poet's world beyond this world has been violated by an event in the real historical world. In the end, the subject of *Love Poems and Elegies* is poetry itself, and the question asked is "What is the value of writing when one is confronted by a dead person?" The answer to that question is discovered in the 1972 sequence, "Orpheus." Here Crichton Smith brings together the themes of his poetry and finds a new perspective.

The Petrarchan sonnet form lends dignity and universality but the movement of the poem is from the world of gods to the world of twentieth-century man, from the ideal to the human. Crichton Smith, like Orpheus, takes a farewell of poetry which transformed and transcended the casual experiences of life.

The legend is a rich one at this stage because its basic themes are the poet's own preoccupations. In the legends, Orpheus is variously musician, prophet, magician and priest of a new religion. His wife, Eurydice, was a dryad whom Aristaeus tried to violate. Escaping, she was bitten by a snake, and died. Orpheus followed her to the underworld and charmed its inhabitants to allow her to return with him back to earth—but on condition that he did not look back at her on the way. Orpheus broke this taboo, and Eurydice became a shade again. The myth has been a rich source to artists since the middle ages, interpreted as allegory and courtly romance. Orpheus has been depicted as the rational man, as an ancient pre-Christian scholar, in a line which runs one through Plato to Moses. The modern playwright has frequently used the myth to explore twentieth-century obsessions: the French dramatist Jean Anouilh's *Eurydice* contrasts the pure young love of Orpheus with the middle-aged world of decay; Tennessee Williams' *Orpheus Descending* takes as its theme the destruction of the artist in the modern, bigoted world of the southern states of America. In film, Cocteau's *Orphée* is perhaps the most well-known treatment: Orpheus returns to the real world to settle happily into cosy domesticity with Eurydice. In poetry, Rilke's "Orpheus, Eurydice and Hermes" presents a Hades which reflects a twentieth-century hell.

The usefulness of the myth to Crichton Smith is clear. Orpheus becomes the artist in a littered, small-town burgh where poems are graffiti scrawled on walls. The dead widowed mother is recast as Eurydice, exploring subtly an Oedipal dimension. The poem takes from the legend Orpheus's experience of separation, and his questioning of his music-making. The sonnets appear to form a dialogue between Orpheus and the god of the underworld, with the divisions between the speakers corresponding to the octave and sestet, apart from two occasions at the end of sections six and seven where the sonnet is divided into two seven-line stanzas. The formality lends order and dignity, yet allows the poet to explore his personal response to his mother's death. It is typical of the superb tensions the poet weaves that he can in this poem abandon the desire which has haunted his work, the desire to engage with the sublime, and instead embrace the everyday, yet choose as a vehicle the most formal of structures, and a classic theme of gods and heroes from the golden age.

In "Orpheus," the poet takes a backward glance over his career in an instinctive, irrevocable movement. When Orpheus glanced back he lost his love for a second, final time. There is the same fresh discovery of loss for the poet himself at the end of this poem; the loss of the self he has created. The point of view, the perspective, has altered. The canvas of his poems includes now his own personal experiences of love and death and such knowledge separates him for ever from the diamond browed one isolated and inviolable in a world beyond this world.

The poem draws together the themes contained in the elegies, opposing the ideal and the human. The god tells Orpheus his loss must be welcomed:

> Always in the air
> her distance will perfect her as Idea.
> Better the far sun of an April day
> than fleshly thunder in the atmosphere.[48]

Cold perfection can no longer satisfy the poet who now questions that distant world beyond this world:

> That is great condemnation,
> to live profoundly and yet much alone.
> To see deeply by a barren passion.[49]

The god replies in the language of the gods, a language of absolutes and ideals:

> If it were possible you would learn to mourn
> even more deeply. Do you never burn
> poems whose language was becoming gray?[50]

Orpheus experiences the impossibility of return. He is shown Eurydice and plays his lute, but the harmony of that "dance of earth and of the air" is lost:

> She seemed not to have changed
> nor he to have changed either as he played.
> And yet her apparition was so strange.
> She didn't fit the music that he made.
> The notes and she were mutually disarranged.[51]

Here is the same discovery made in the elegies: human experience never fits the ideals and paradigms with which we constantly try to master it. Uppermost is the idea of a misfit between life and art as Orpheus has always understood it.

The god insists that his voice has never been other, but has been Orpheus's own voice, speaking his innermost desire that "You wished that she should die." Orpheus and the god, then, seem not two distinct voices, but spring from impulses from the one mind: the poet for whom art could be neatly separated from life, and the poet who has grown suspicious of the neat frame, who has discovered its limitations and distortions.

If Crichton Smith's movement away from his Calvinist roots has been halted by the death of his mother, if that event discovers him outcast, so too is he outcast from his world beyond this world. The new knowledge means that world is forever denied him. Yet to stay with the god, in that world beyond this world, would offer quietude. The god inhabits an inhuman world, which offers essential perfection. Orpheus sees around him only vanity fair, "the beggar seated in alternate gloom / and negligent neon." The reference to the beggar contains within it all the references the writer has made to his experience of seeing a beggar in Aberdeen railway station when he was seventeen and had left Lewis for the first time. His shock revealed how strong were the roots of his Lewis culture. In the city of Aberdeen, such beggars were abandoned. In Lewis, they would have been absorbed into, and cared for by, the community. The beggar, then, produces within him a gut-reaction which tells him he is a Lewisman, rooted in that culture. The experience encroaches on the neat frame which separates art from life. To stay with the god, to rest in an inhuman world, "to lay aside my lyre and sleep at last" is a death wish and denied by the god.

Orpheus is abandoned in the "ugly and adulterated waste" of slums, broken windows and graffiti: "There were poems / chalked on the flaking walls, misspelt, ill-worded."[52] Graffiti is the expression of the art of the people, not of the gods. It is not the music Pluto played, "such music as the zodiac / is made of" but such music as the world allows, flawed, and imperfect. This wasteland infects Orpheus's art:

> and his lyre clouded as with greenish slime
> and all the brilliant strings appeared corroded
> by it and the monotony of time.[53]

The "greenish slime" corrodes but "as with" and "appeared" defer that judgement and allow space for new assessment.

The poem ends with images which suggest baptism and rebirth and Orpheus's recognition of bittersweet gain, yet these are inscribed on a human, domestic canvas. A white-vested man washes, a child blows bubbles, Elvis Presley and Valentino parade as heroes. Here is a new poetry:

> And so his lyre had a graver heavier tone
> as if containing all the possible grains
> that can be found in marble or in stone.
> What he had lost was the sweet and random strains
> which leaped obliquely from the vast unknown

concordances and mirrors but the gains,
though seeming sparser, were more dearly won.[54]

The rhymes here enact a new restriction and limitation: "tone," "stone," "grains," "strains" and "gains" insist on the limited canvas. "The sweet and random strains" are relinquished. The "mirror" of his early poems reflected back an identity created in opposition to the poet's background. Here, "mirror" is linked with "marble" and "stone." Coming after "graver" they echo the elegies, suggesting gravestones, unreadable, reflecting nothing. The creation of an identity constructed in and by language has been violated by something outside his language. The gaze of the death's head which made the poet stutter has been absorbed into his discourse. "Vast unknown concordances" once offered the poet a discourse which promised an identity separated from his background. Their counterpart must now be admitted. The gravestone already contains "all the possible grains." Reflected light, movement and unpredictability are contrasted with a set pattern ingrained in stone. The god and Orpheus represent two poets, then. The diamond browed early poet, inviolate, and Orpheus, who is now possessed of a terrible knowledge. At the end of the poem, Orpheus stands poised, confronting loss and gain, recognising fully that the identity of poet is no longer a free act of will, but is created from something already set down.

Notes

1. Lorne Macintyre, "Poet in Bourgeois Land," *Scottish International* (September 1971), 22-28 (p. 27).
2. *The Ambassadors* hangs in the National Gallery.
3. Carol Gow, "An Interview with Iain Crichton Smith," *Scottish Literary Journal* 17:2 (November 1990), 43-57 (p. 55).
4. "The Highland Element in my English Work," *Scottish Literary Journal*, 4 (1977), 47-60 (p. 51).
5. Robert Lowell, *Poems 1938-1949* (London: Faber & Faber, 1964), p. 18.
6. Patrick Cosgrave, *The Public Poetry of Robert Lowell* (London: Gollancz, 1970), p. 89.
7. *Saltire Review*, 4 (1957), p. 55.
8. Reprinted in *Sea Sorrow* (Stornoway: *Gazette*, 1972), p. 30.
9. *Ibid.*, p. 31.
10. *Ibid.*, p. 34.
11. *Thistles and Roses* (London: Eyre & Spottiswoode, 1961), p. 45.
12. *Sea Sorrow*, p. 34.
13. "The Highland Element in my English Work," p. 51.
14. *The Exiles* (Manchester: Carcanet, 1984), p. 44.
15. *Ibid.*, p. 45.
16. John Blackburn, *A Writer's Journey*, booklet and five cassette recordings (Edinburgh: Moray College of Education, 1981).

17. "The Highland Element in my English Work," p. 53.
18. "Between Sea and Moor," in *As I Remember* (London: Hale, 1979), edited by Maurice Lindsay, pp. 107-121 (p. 116).
19. *Selected Poems 1955-1980* (Edinburgh: Macdonald, 1981), p. 4.
20. *Love Poems and Elegies* (London: Gollancz, 1972), p. 12.
21. *Ibid.*, p. 11.
22. *Ibid.*, p. 12.
23. *Ibid.*, p. 13.
24. *Ibid.*, p. 16.
25. *Ibid.*
26. *Ibid.*, p. 14.
27. *Ibid.*, p. 17.
28. *Ibid.*
29. *Ibid.*, p. 21.
30. *Ibid.*, p. 22.
31. *Ibid.*, p. 31.
32. *Ibid.*, p. 29.
33. *Ibid.*
34. "Poetry, Passion and Political Consciousness," *Scottish International* (May 1970), pp. 10-16 (10).
35. *Love Poems and Elegies,* p. 34; p. 35.
36. *Ibid.*, p. 36.
37. *Ibid.*
38. *Ibid.*, p. 32.
39. *Ibid.*
40. *Ibid.*, p. 38.
41. "The Future of Gaelic Literature," in *Transactions of the Gaelic Society of Inverness*, 43 (1961), 172-180 (p. 176-177).
42. *Ibid.*
43. *Love Poems and Elegies*, p. 41.
44. *Ibid.*, p. 60.
45. *Ibid.*, p. 53.
46. *The Complete Poems of Hugh MacDiarmid*, Vol. 1, edited by Michael Grieve and W. R. Aitken (London: Penguin, 1985), p. 14.
47. *Love Poems and Elegies*, p. 50.
48. *Orpheus and Other Poems* (Preston: Akros, 1974), p. 10.
49. *Ibid.*
50. *Ibid.*
51. *Ibid.*, p. 11.
52. *Ibid.*, p. 13.
53. *Ibid.*
54. *Ibid.*, p. 14.

G

CHAPTER FIVE

Crusoe

If identity for the poet can no longer be perceived as a free act of writing but must contain what is already written, Crichton Smith must confront his Lewis background. Yet the Lewis text is hostile and threatening because it seems to offer only definition and limitation, the antithesis to the freedom of the poet to write himself:

> one is known as the person one is, forever. One's parents are known, one's grandparents are known, one is in an assigned position.[1]

The assigned position of "son" assumes overwhelming significance in *Love Poems and Elegies* because it is the death of his mother which violates his world beyond this world: he is at that moment both assigned the irrevocable position of son and abandoned, eternally orphaned. It is significant that in the volumes which follow *Love Poems and Elegies* Crichton Smith avoids the confrontation with the Lewis background to embrace instead the figure of the outcast. *The Notebooks of Robinson Crusoe* and *In The Middle* offer a crucible in which a new poetry is formed.

"The Notebooks of Robinson Crusoe," a long sequence which gives the volume its title, insists on a fresh start, a clean page, virgin territory. The persona of Robinson Crusoe, a creatively logical choice, offers a rich vehicle for Crichton Smith's exploration of self and of language:

> He links with some of my own obsessions, the examination of isolation, musings about the problems of language (since I myself am creatively bilingual), and the idea of the poster hero (or the comic book hero).[2]

Crichton Smith's Orpheus was abandoned by the god in a poem which moved steadily from the world of gods to the world of men. Crusoe is removed from such a choice, left to create his own world on his desert island. As Crusoe creates his world, the poet shapes a new identity, exploring and elucidating the contradictions between the tragic and the comic, the sacred and the profane, the text and the life.

Crusoe's list of resources rescued from the ship includes one axe, twelve hatchets and twelve knives, tools of survival with which to carve his new world: "To be busy without mirror. / To let the day invent itself."[3] The commitment is to fact, not fancy, the reality, not the myth, the life, not the text. Crusoe carves his world on a bare landscape with basic tools. The "notebook" form of the poems suggests a similar minimalist approach, many of the poems content to offer lists, attempting to set down a language linked to a concrete reality, sign glued to referent. "Without mirror" and "to let the day invent itself" suggest the possibility of discovering identity without accepting either the mirror of his poetry or of his society. Yet the tools in Crusoe's hands belie the fresh start: the face reflected in the axe insists that Crusoe is a socially-constructed inheritor.

Avoiding reflection is impossible. Other things are brought besides tools. Crusoe carries with him other baggage. Memories and dreams disturb and prompt the desire:

O that I were a man without memory, a machine renewed by the days, a tree that forgets its autumn leaves, its winter dispossessions.[4]

But Crusoe brings his past with him. He remembers Margaret, and a love affair that has the bittersweet quality of the love poems in *Love Poems and Elegies* where the loved one reflected back to him his own anxieties and his own flawed existence. Yet "with knife carved Margaret" offers an idealised figure, "breasts outthrust, meditative, of herself: pinning her wooden hair back, looking down."[5] On the island of Lewis, the young boy was chastised for carving wooden hens because they were frowneed upon as graven images. Margaret here is not a copy of the real Margaret but "of herself" and complete. On this island, art has no justification save itself.

Comparison between Margaret and the wooden figure reveals only difference. Here on his island, Crusoe confronts his reflection in the mirror to discover that the apparent harmony of self and image cannot conceal disunity:

I propped the mirror against a rock. At once the sky entered it, the sea, and my unshaven wolfish famished face.
I seethed the soap busily into my beard and grasping the cut throat began to reap, my real hand and the image moving together.[6]

The myth of entry is exposed here. The sky has always already entered. In the mirror, the "I" is situated. Around him is a world of sky and sea. The image in the mirror that stares back offers "Robinson Crusoe." The verbs "seethed," "grasping," bring their reward in "reap." He is the agent, his will is exercised here. "Grasping the cut throat" is nicely ambiguous: it is at once the open razor he uses to shave, and the throat of Crusoe, cut because language itself, Crichton Smith has written, is a trap in which the writer bleeds.[7] Unity is promised in "my real hand and the image moving together," the perfect harmony of something that fits perfectly with its image. But suddenly "a voice" intrudes:

"Abolish the sea and the sky, the beasts and the
birds and the fish and the rigging half buried in sand and brine."
The cut-throat of its own will descended to my throat as the
silence of the world prolonged itself.[8]

The hyphen used here limits "cut-throat" more closely towards the interpretation of razor, but "cut-throat" and "my throat" evoke the real face of Robinson Crusoe and the reflection in the mirror. A sense of self is fractured here: the self in the mirror, the self created in the mirror of his poems through language, urges Crusoe to "abolish" what is around him, to free himself from time and place, from the assigned position. Yet that can be achieved only by breaking the mirror which will destroy the image Crusoe has of himself, or by committing suicide. A sense of self, of wholeness, comes only through being situated in a certain place at a certain time and yet that moment when accident becomes significance, when the individual perceives self in the mirror of his community, is also the moment of disharmony, fracture and alienation. The reflection in the mirror, and Crusoe's face, are therefore locked into a relationship. For the poet, the reflection in the mirror of Calvinist Lewis and of bourgeois Scotland has always revealed only disharmony. That disjunction leads to an examination of language, of self, and to the discovery that the "I" does not fit the subject but is alienated through the mirror, the text which elucidates it.
The silence is broken by the "I" who insists

"In no other face shall ever be duplicated those grieving eyes, that nose, the mouth at whose corners radiate lines of injustice and petulance."[9]

Is this a threat to destroy the "other face," the false reflection? "Grieving," "injustice" and "petulance" suggest a usurped "I." Yet "radiate" brings us back to a Hamlet figure, whose "injury is not an injury *to* me, it *is* me."[10] A sense of unity of identity is achieved at that moment of alienation, usurpation. "I said" and "I cried" confuse as image and self become confused and the "wolf" which howls is answered by another "hollow wolf." This confusion is held steady with the word "steadily" in

Steadily I reaped, clearing the undergrowth, clarifying the lines of the face, elucidating its text.
It is no mean novel sensationally hot from the printers: it is true Bible, responsible. On it shall all words be printed.[11]

"Began to reap" culminates in "reap." "Lines," "text," "no mean novel" and "all words be printed" accepts "homo textual" and the individual constructed in and by his language.[12] Yet "novel" is contrasted with "Bible" and "mean" with "true": oppositions which fall into the categories of the "vast unknown concordances" and "all the possible grains" of the Orpheus poem and offer the same hegemony—a cold, sober language taking precedence over sensational heat, truth over lies. But significantly it comes through a new analysis. The act of shaving is an act of criticising. Clearing the undergrowth finds its parallel in Crusoe's work on the island. The island is his mirror and his labour creates both subject and object. The "I" is bound up with text, but there is an urge to abandon a language which obscures and find a language which reveals self. Crichton Smith has spoken about his decision to abandon a "dandyish" language: "where one is sort of flourishing the language and creating such a dazzle that nobody knows what's going on underneath it." Such language appears to create a self somewhere between a Prospero and a charlatan, the poet as poseur:

> Looking back on it now it looks so false, you know? It was part of that kind of glitter and knowingness about things which I sort of repulsed at a certain stage because it didn't seem to correlate with the experiences of people, ordinary people, in a way. . . . I think in a sense it was going back to . . . a kind of Calvinist honesty . . . to see things as they are, you know, rather than having that kind of dazzling light.[13]

The imagery of reaping and clearing, clarifying and elucidating, suggests strongly the stripping away of an identity which somehow obscures in an attempt to find out "what's going on underneath." "Mean" has another pairing in "all." "On it shall all words be printed" suggests a full commitment to homo textual, to language, but Crichton Smith's expression "Calvinist honesty" illuminates the authority of the word "Bible." It is *the* book, which contains all wisdom and suggests in part the idea of speaking on oath, telling the whole truth and nothing but the truth, and perhaps also the need for the identity of the poet to connect with Iain Crichton Smith the man brought up on the island of Lewis, the man born in a certain place at a certain time, and a demand for the kind of honesty he recognises in the Gaelic poet Sorley MacLean:

> One has the feeling of integrity, that his life and his work are not separate and that what he really thinks about himself is in the poetry. I mean he doesn't make himself actually better than he is in the poetry.[14]

101

The death of Crichton Smith's mother has revealed to the poet the separation of life and work, of the self of his poetry and the self brought up on Calvinist Lewis and it is this disunity which needs to be explored and worked through in the poems in this volume. The poet who confronts his face in the mirror while shaving confronts a recognition of disharmony, and the commitment is made to the elucidation of the text, so that life and work, self and image, become one. The poem ends on a note of doubleness—not quite disharmony or fracture, but partnership and a note of redemption: "To the end, I said: to the shadow dogging my heels, to my scrubbed pearl, to my obedient hand."[15] "To the end" of the life, or the book which is the text of the life, the hand will be obedient, the hand of the author, the writing hand, no longer threatening to destroy, to silence.

The bible and the book echo the texts in which the young boy on the island of Lewis first perceived self; the Bible and a *Penguin New Writing*. For the boy, the two texts offered choices. Here these appear no longer choices, but promise a unified text. Yet the partnership is a curious one, as "dogging" and "shadow" reveal. The Lewis background has always been the antithesis to his poetry, and in many ways it is hard not to see this as a positive catalyst, providing a basis for a poetry of opposition. Crichton Smith, however, perceives his Free Church background in negative terms: "I feel that it has done my own writing no good at all, except as something to fight against."[16] The desire, therefore, for a "Calvinist honesty" in his work is a dangerous one. The Lewis background which produces the man, which gives him his roots, is hostile soil because of the religion which nourishes it. Recognition of that dangerous relationship and the need "to fight against it" comes in a poem about a gunfight between "I" and "a man in a black hat," in a scene from the Westerns of Crichton Smith's childhood reading. The man in the black hat is also representative of the "hard black hatted" men from "Highland Sunday," an early poem in which the poet's church-goers are drowned in the sensuous, "dandyish" language of the early poetry in *The White Noon*.[17] Here the black hatted figure is recast in a scene from the Western "High Noon." The "I" is the dreamer and poet, the black hatted man the Calvinist opponent. The "I" can no longer choose one over the other. The idea of duel suggests "dual" and the doubleness of the "I." The outcome of the identity of the survivor is left in doubt, revealing the illusion of wholeness:

> If I could fire
> just once more
> I'd know who fell.[18]

The poet is left asking "who?"

The desire to create afresh, to take upon himself the writing of the story of his own life, is strong. In "Today I Wished To Write A Story," Crusoe contemplates a story of his own experiences on the island which would show him running to meet his rescuer who "would run through him bone and sinew to the other side," imagery which suggests apparent unity but, like the mirror image, offers a created, and false, harmony. What Crusoe will create is an "I" who has no substance, who has become mere or more text. Instead of writing afresh his own story, Crusoe opens his Bible to make the discovery that his history has already been written:.

> written in faded ink on
> the leaf before Genesis the words, "To my dearest son from
> his mother."
> I could not elucidate the date.[19]

Crusoe opens his Bible before the beginning, before Genesis. But there is already something written before that beginning: "To my dearest son from his mother." Opening the Bible before Genesis confronts the desire to go behind the beginning which Wittgenstein suggests is impossible: "to place ourselves outside the world and to see where and how it begins."[20] Taking up the position of outcast, freed from the Gaelic matriarch, Crusoe inhabits a desert island in an attempt to find a starting point before the beginning, a starting point which can begin to answer the question "who?". Yet before the beginning, something is written. The text has already inscribed him son. The inscription suggests the words of baptism, and pulls in the text of John 1, i, "In the beginning was the Word." The discovery here is that identity is given, imposed by language. "I could not elucidate the date" subverts the placing of ourselves outside the world and outside the word.

Crichton Smith's heroes, the diamond browed one, Hamlet, Orpheus, have allowed him a certain stance. His bilingualism has offered him two linguistic worlds. Yet "who?" can no longer be anwered by any of these partial definitions. When God calls to Abraham and he answers "Here I am," the weight of the description in that statement falls not on "I" but on "here." Abraham finds an answer to who I am by answering to God the father. W. H. Auden's remarks on naming reveal also that the child's sense of identity is created as it is addressed by its parents and that the child is firstly "thou" before it is "I": "we respond and obey before we can summon and command."[21]

This is the fate Crusoe is forced to acknowledge. Identity is bound up with community. Alone on the island he is homo textual. The wish to write his own story, the discovery that he is already written, reveal only that the subject of the story, and Crusoe the castaway, are each textual constructions.

On the island of Lewis, the poet was in an assigned position. On his desert island, too, identity is always assigned by language, by the word. Yet new territory has been won. In Crusoe, the poet finds a comic book hero who allows him to combine the things which he has often kept separate in the compartments of "art" and "life," the sacred and the profane. Inscribed in the comic books, he takes his place alongside Dan Dare and Desperate Dan:

> Today I climbed the hills of the imagination, hearing in the hollow canyons a voice crying ROBINSON CRUSOE and knew that in my shabby skins I walked with my true companions, smelling the very pages in which my accident became significant purpose.[22]

In Crichton Smith's novel, *Goodbye Mr Dixon*, his novelist hero is drawn to a comic world but feels it shameful:

> Tom liked the comics for the same reason as he liked jazz, their spontaneity, their unpredictable nature and also their bright colours, their vulgar yellows and crimsons. But he would never have told anyone that he loved reading them, that Desperate Dan was one of his heroes. . . . He felt that he ought to be reading better books, . . . and that he shouldn't be dwelling too often in that irresponsible world of crazy hosepipes and flung pies and dishelmeted policemen, all falling about in a crimson sky.[23]

Tom apparently subscribes to the Renaissance hierarchy of high, low and middle styles. He regards the love of comics as shameful because it is the world of comedy where "everything came right in the end." In that anarchic and irresponsible world, there is no part for the tragic hero. Tom, like almost all of Crichton Smith's protagonists, makes the journey from a self-consciously élitist literary figure, the hero of his own tragedy, towards a figure who is more open to the world, its ordinariness and simplicities, its vulgarities and diversities. The comics therefore, offer Crusoe an anarchic world, no longer shameful and irresponsible, but offering "bright colours" instead of the black text of Lewis, and "dishelmeted policemen" instead of Law. Inscribed in this text, Crusoe recognises his part. "Accident" is set against "significant." "Significant" here means carrying a sign. These oppositions suggest the accident of a fragmented self and the significance of a unified sense of identity perceived in the mirror of the poems. In the heroes of the comic books, Crichton Smith finds an identity which promises a more truthful reflection.

The poet's earlier tragic heroes of Hamlet and Orpheus were created by the mirror of Scottish culture. Hamlet's identity was created by a reaction against the patriarchal "law" and language of a petty bourgeois society. The specular imagery in the Hamlet poems is a grotesque distortion because society is the mirror in which the individual sees himself reflected back whole only when he is at home there. Orpheus is formed specifically in relation to the Gaelic Matriarch. The bourgeois patriarch and the Gaelic matriarch are constructed to give birth to these figures of Hamlet and Orpheus. The construction walks abroad, shadowing Oedipus, rebelling against the father figure and, desiring to claim the mother as the loved one, locked into the tragic dénouement. The death of his mother is a terrible liberation for the poet, casting him out, setting him free, making redundant the script he has written. Yet a fresh script needs a starting point from which to begin again.

On the island Crusoe can explore new scripts. He finds identity no longer with the tragic figures of his early work but with the absurd heroes of the comics, "where art unexpectedly flowers from the vulgar." If Tom guiltily read his comics, Crusoe satiates his appetite gluttonously, reading a "bunch of old comics . . . the Victor and the Wizard, the Dandy and the Rover." Here he can listen to the "gossip of the unphilosophical":

> "Bark. Yap. Yap."
> "Yap. Yap. Grr. Woof."
> "Aargh."[24]

These are the "legends of the comic misfits" and their language, a shared joke where inarticulate sounds articulate meaning, somehow seems to provide that beginning before the beginning Wittgenstein suggests could only be inarticulate. They are "the colours before God," before Genesis, before "In the beginning was the Word." Here is a poet delivered into an anarchic and unpredictable world, celebrating with a libertine, liberated poetry. If the answer to who? can be defined only by accepting an assigned position, by where?, the poet can now answer "Here":

> Here at Marathon I sit holding my comics above the salt concentration and diffusion, forgetting the tragic legions, the mussel-coloured armour of the hoplites.[25]

The "salt concentration and diffusion" partakes of everything that the sea has represented in literature. For Crichton Smith, more particularly, the sea is "monster and creator."[26] The meaning of the phrase therefore must take account of that duality. "Salt" is often the word used to represent all that the poet finds threatening to his work. Salt may add flavour but Crichton Smith's comments on his Gaelic background deny that it enriches his work. It is seen as destructive. "Salt" here is rather salt rubbed into the wound in the side, the wound of the Promethean poet. The image is one of precarious survival, of the triumph of the comic book heroes over the "tragic legions."

Inscribed in the comic book, Crichton Smith finds a text which combines art and the vulgar. Crusoe's desire to "nail my 'sea' to sea, my 'hill' to hill" reflects on signifier and signified, on the arbitrary connection to the referent. He asks "how can the immigrant lay down his rules?"[27] Inscribed in the comic books, he can abandon rules and embrace anarchy. On the island, Pretty Poll the parrot takes up Crusoe's name: "Crusoe . . . Cruise . . . Crew," reflecting back to Crusoe his obsession with a return to the society implicated in "cruise" and "crew."[28] Poll takes up Crusoe's name and allows language to slip and slide but "accident becomes significant purpose."

Crusoe's companion, Friday, is also introduced to Crusoe's language. Friday is his "comic shadow," an "imperfect me" and provides an opposition to the superior Crusoe: "I adopt poses, the wise father, the artistic creator, the elder brother, the good friend."[29] Identity for the "I" here depends on Friday, on the relationship he adopts towards him, but they remain poses because Friday as mirror reveals not the imagined reciprocity of the mirror, but the actuality of one-way reflection. Friday refuses to allow the hegemony, the colonising through language:

> I lodge my imperturbable rainbow in his skies.
> He aborts my technology. He sings incomprehensible songs.
> I do not learn his world.[30]

Friday is the anarchic figure who disrupts the rules. The "imperturbable rainbow" is Crusoe's language, language which has drawn boundaries between tragedy and comedy. "Lodge" argues both for tenancy, and a temporary quality. If the rainbow is "imperturbable" it will become a dead language. Friday brings anarchy and life:

> His shiny black humorous face looks up at me, idiot being, Black Minstrel of this drama, comic relief in my classical tragedy.[31]

"This drama," "my classical tragedy," provides a script for the poet now which includes the "black ministrel," and "comic relief." Constructing his other, Crusoe finds his tragedy in the mirror of the "idiot being," the master finds his mastery in the non-reciprocal mirror of the slave.

Crusoe's text, his identity, was to be "no mean novel" but "true Bible," but even that purity is threatened in "Friday's Fragments" when Friday takes up Crusoe's prayer. Just as Poll took up language and allowed it to become slippery and unpredictable, so too Friday's prayer becomes humorous and blasphemous. Language misbehaves but it also comes alive:

Our fat
her
witch
heart
in hev-
en
hallo-
wed
bee
thy
name
hallo
wed
bee
thy
hallo . . .
Thy
king
dumb
come
thy
king
dumb
come . . .[32]

Crichton Smith's exploration of self and language leads to celebration of the anarchic. Isolated on the desert island, he still cannot escape the assigned position; the words written on the flyleaf of his Bible name him son, the tools Crusoe works with tie him to his role of heir, just as the language the poet uses is inherited. The fixed identity, the written part that could not be rejected, led to the birth of the tragic heroes of his poems. Yet the discovery made on the island is that identity is constructed through text. The arbitrariness of language reflects the arbitrariness of identity, cause for celebration because it allows the script to be altered. Language is finally seen not as a trap, but rather as a net:

This I say:
One man cannot warm the world.
This I say:
The world of one man is different from the world of many men.
This I say:
Without the net, the sweetest fish are tasteless.[33]

"This I say" foregrounds textuality. Taken together with the aphoristic flavour of the statements they suggest not a truth, but a truth-for-now, a new basis from which to begin, which welcomes the accidental nature of identity.

When Crusoe leaves his island, it is the abandonment of a part, a role, which parallels Hamlet's death, centre-stage, in *Hamlet In Autumn*. Hamlet discovers that the distorting glass finally reflects nothing. Crusoe, too, is locked in a solipsistic isolation. A quotation from the 1987 novel, *In The Middle Of The Wood*, offers illumination here. Ralph Simmons, recovered from a mental breakdown, says:

> He knew suddenly why Hamlet needed Horatio as a witness, why Horatio had to be left behind to tell the truth as he saw it, to explain the extraordinary pattern of events, the murders, the accidents. The most terrible thing of all would be to be in a world without witnesses, a Robinson Crusoe on an island. That in a sense was what he had been.[34]

"Homo textual" is a Robinson Crusoe in a "world beyond this world" without witnesses. Hamlet needs Horatio to tell his story, just as Crusoe must rejoin the world, because each needs verification, a witness to the story, the *text* of the self. "To explain the pattern" and "the accidents" is to transform accident into significant purpose. Samuel Beckett's plays and novels have continually explored the fictions by which we live, and his protagonists are constantly threatened by silence. Crichton Smith experiences the crisis that Beckett experiences: identity is bound up with text, with saying. Without a witness, it is simply accident. Crusoe returns to the world because without it he has no significance. The created self needs the mirror of society in order to perceive his sign. Yet the mirror which offers a sense of self also alienates and distorts. The illusion of harmony is revealed in the image of the face which "swells like a jester's"

> I shall leave my bare island, simple as poison, to enter the equally poisonous world of Tiberius, where there are echoes and reflections, a Hall of Mirrors in which my face like all faces swells like a jester's in a world without sense.[35]

The image from the earlier *From Bourgeois Land* of the Hall of Mirrors is redefined: mirrors not only distort but rob the individual of his individuality. The tragic hero of the solitary drama awaits his new role in the crowd of existence. He has a choice, however. He can remain "in the middle of the dark wood" or he can leave for the "communal inferno where we feed on each other"—a choice between the desert island of a "world beyond this world" without a witness, and the historical world which must include the Lewis text. In a play on Sartre's "Hell is other people," Crusoe's hell is language itself as he hears "the same phrase repeated over and over: Language is other people."[36]

There is no alter-ego in *In The Middle*, no reflection in the mirror, no god and no literary figure, because the discovery made in *The Notebooks of Robinson Crusoe* is that "who" is a question which is exhausted and ultimately collapses into "where." Phrases such as "seen from here" and "where I wished to be" speak of position, not identity, because the "I" is a text, written before he can write.[37] The quest for identity results not in "who" but "where": finding out where the self is inscribed. *In The Middle* suggests that identity cannot be worked out on the desert island, only in the middle. Crichton Smith has inhabited the skins of tragic hero and comic book hero: *In The Middle* describes an I who takes his bearing from both these positions but fully occupies neither.

In the opening poem, the poet himself exists outside the discourses which surround him. He waits, like others, in a doctor's surgery. A group of patients read horoscopes and love stories, texts which insist on a fixed fate. The receptionist is a decalogist: "No dogs permitted. / On Saturdays, Emergency Cases Only."[38] The doctor offers medical platitudes and the reassurance: "And if you die, why that's nothing. / Plenty of people have died and been buried also."[39] "Plenty of people" deposes the tragic hero and places him in the crowd. Yet there is something to be said for the doctor's prescription of "red and black" pills. Red and black stand for the extremities of Crichton Smith's register: red frequently represents an exposure to the raw, accidental and sometimes overpowering flux of life, black represents Calvinism, Law and death. Both stand as the antithesis to his poetry. The poem ends with water imagery:

So I went away and stared into the water.
People were passing by and some were laughing.
They all flowed with the stream in their coloured clothes.[40]

"So I went away" combines a simple way of moving the narrative forward and the echo of Biblical prose, heard because this "surgery" offers a metaphor for a world where people wait to be redeemed, wait to answer to the word of God—to be assigned position. The banalities of the doctor are nevertheless true: "It is true what he said: There's no cure for it." But the last two lines, "What is in the water but more water? / If you close your eyes, you hear the endless footsteps" allow the conditional "if" and the caesura in the second line to position an I poised between the crowd and his own isolation.[41] The poet wanders between heaven and hell here, rooted in neither.

On the island, Crusoe's language was "imperturbable": refused by Friday, mimicked by Poll the Parrot, it remained closed, limited to

Crusoe's meanings. The poet of *In The Middle* explores the imperturbability of the discourse of patristic writing, taking up the discourse as an outsider, and revealing how it is imperturbable because of the label that comes attached to it, instructing the reader how to read, attempting to limit the areas of response so that there is an obvious position established for the reader at which the discourse is intelligible.

Two poems take as their starting point the language of religion and expose it to a literal, not metaphorical, reading. Patristic writing must be read in a certain way. The example quoted earlier from Genesis 22:11 of Abraham's answer to God, "Here I am," will make the point. We do not start wondering where "here" is because we obey the instructions of the text to read it not as a spatial term, but a moral term.[42] We are aware of these rules governing the language of devotion when we read the Bible. Thomas Merill has suggested that the nouns in the 23rd Psalm, pasture, water, path, valley, table, oil and house make ethical and non-theological sense so long as we ignore the initial, controlling metaphor, "The Lord is my Shepherd." He calls this the "semantic tyranny of God."[43] Reading patristic writings we accede to this tyranny and obey the rules. The poet here is a misplaced outcast, caught in the middle, outside the rules of this discourse. In "Hail Mary" and "Prepare Ye The Way of The Lord" he flouts the rules, and has fun with the language.

In "Hail Mary" the poet takes up the phrase of devotion and ignores the semantic tyranny, audaciously hailing Mary as if he is some domineering passer-by who accosts her on the street or the supermarket. She is compared to the mother figure offered as a role-model to women in television advertising: "so busy / among clothes and saucepans, rinsing the world clean."[44] "Rinsing the world clean" both links these women to and separates them from Mary: she washing away sins in a spiritual world, they attacking more practical stains in a more practical way. Heaven and hell, body and soul, are binaries which are allowed to collapse here. The woman who inhabits the world worries about keeping up with the Joneses:

> If you've got the right outfit for the party,
> the right lipstick for the seventies,
> the right kind of body for the ads—
> as for the soul that's something else again.[45]

"The right kind of body" is a reminder that this apparently ordinary woman in the ads is really a star posing as an ordinary housewife. She is an icon. "The soul" finds its counterpart in "body" in a horse-and-cart link, but the sudden deliberate vagueness of the last line allows it to float free of the previous lines, not in an achieved leap towards illumination as in earlier poems but as a gesture towards something inexpressible. "That's something else again" signals towards surplus, but exploration is shut down by the judgement on Mary:

> I think the soul makes you rather dull.
> You should brighten up a bit. It's fruitless
> to remain so high up there on a cloud
> and not among our labour-saving kitchens.[46]

The speaker is firmly entrenched in the practical yet never-never land portrayed in advertising for kitchens, soaps and detergents where all stains can be washed away. It is not a world for poets.

In the Bible, when Gabriel speaks to Mary, she is hailed as the mother of Jesus, and set apart from her domestic identity:

> And the angel came unto her, and said Hail, thou that art highly favoured, the Lord is with thee: blessed art thou among women. And when she saw him, she was troubled at his saying and cast in her mind what manner of salutation this should be.[47]

This "manner of salutation" assigns Mary's position as "blessed" and set apart from other women. The poet's salutation is also an act which assigns position, this time placing Mary firmly "among women," among the stereotypes of housewives. The devotional recitation is removed from the language of devotion, broken free of the rules governing that discourse and from the protection afforded by its rules, and opened up to new interpretations. Mary is the Mary of the biblical text visited by Gabriel, and she is also Mary of the pots and pans. She is the archetype "mother" in both a text of devotion and a text of advertising. Her identity slips as she moves between Heaven and the hell of everyday, enclosed by neither.

"Prepare ye the way of the Lord" also flouts the semantic tyranny of "Lord" in the opening line, to continue: "put pebbles on it, / and after that tar."[48] The poet plunges on with a literal, not metaphorical, interpretation. The "way" in patristic writing is different from the "way" in a directional sign like "way out" only because it is protected by special rules and conventions which we obey. But what happens if we pull aside such protection from the language? It flowers into new and unexpected life, shimmering between the two meanings. The poet "In The Surgery" needed pills which were "red and black" for health. An involvement with the everyday is complex, both destructive and creative. The lines above bend into new meaning, but Crichton Smith here seems to be deflecting the position from which the text is intelligible from a heaven to hell, from a "world beyond this world" to the everyday, in order to prove how meagre such a text can be. In the second half of the following verse, however, "and the roses be seen

111

in the mirrors / when the cars have passed them," the poem shifts again from the straightforward, everyday reading towards metaphor. "Roses" and "mirrors" are words from the earlier poetry, from the "world beyond this world" and a language over which the heroes of Prometheus, Hamlet and Orpheus exercised a semantic tyranny. The lines offer a metaphor for a new kind of poetry: one apparently more simple, more straightforward, but yet which offers something half-caught, reflected to a backward glance: a poetry which exists "in the middle."

"The Elite" offers a less-positive assessment. The dinosaurs "got on with being dinosaurs" while the rain came down because they simply could not be otherwise. In this poem, the first line of the last stanza, "grief fades quickly through the world's leaves," offers words which seem strangely alien in the discourse in which they occur; their rhythms and cadence are different, too, like the "rain" of common sense which drowns reflection suddenly dying out.[49] It is poetic discourse, yet unprotected by the text which surrounds it. One line fights for survival. The poem speaks of extinction, dead leaves, and offers up one line, like a new leaf on a dead branch. Yet it is important to recognise that this one line does not carry the whole meaning and weight of the poem. It is not a line pointing to illumination or epiphany. In a sense, the poet seems not to be behind the line—it is thrown in, "in the middle," to survive or not.

Drawing aside the protection from patristic writing, Crichton Smith opens up its discourse, and in this process reveals how he has opened up his own poetry to the world. The new poetry Crichton Smith is writing seems to be a working out of the conflicts he elucidated in MacDiarmid's poetry:

> At a certain stage MacDiarmid was willing or was compelled to open himself out to life and being of an extremely sensitive nature he was nearly destroyed by it. To have sustained such insights would have been annihilating. Yet he wished to retain such insights for he knew that as a poet he was dependent on them. He was being more extreme than one has the power to be—and survive. But to survive—was that worth it when one could survive only as a bourgeois and lead a living death?[50]

The "dinosaur" who kept on being a dinosaur did not survive. Yet the price of survival may be too high. For Crichton Smith, the engagement of the poet with the hell of everyday is essential yet potentially destructive: Crusoe leaves his island because he needs a witness, yet knows the world to which he journeys is "equally poisonous." The image Crichton Smith finds for the new poetry he is writing is one of conflict between predatory and passive forces:

> when the red sun rises, raw and ominous,
> with its grained angry ore and it sees the moon
> hated and indolent, ghosting possessed land.[51]

In conflict here is the early poetry of moons and vases and a new, perhaps destructive, force. "Ghosting possessed land" suggests the poetry of *The Long River*, which echoed the English poets of his reading and which was permeated with images of exile and ghosts, recalling Auden. "Ghosting" offers a shadowy identity and the idea of imitation and reflection; "grained" carries with it a meaning long in the making; the red sun stands for life, for what is already written, the antithesis to the creative act. Identity is in conflict here.

In "Painting The Walls," the poet makes use of red and yellow to describe different identities: "A man in a yellow room is different from / a man in a red room."[52] Their use here is a mark of the poet's confidence in the distinctive spectrum he has developed. In Crichton Smith's poetry, "black" stands for the Calvinist ideology against which he sets the white and yellow of his moons and daffodils. Yellow moves from being the colour of the free daffodil towards a colour of crisis and disturbance. Red stands for a life-giving, yet feared, flux. In this volume an interesting new colour appears. "The Purple Bucket" renegotiates the earlier "The Black Jar" which reflected on Wallace Stevens' "Anecdote of the Jar." The jar has become a bucket. Crichton Smith has commented, "There are times when one brings a poem home like a bucket full of water making sure that none of it spills."[53] Instead of a Wordsworthian "spontaneous overflow of powerful feelings," the poet offers a metaphor of containment, and an absence of surplus.[54] Yet here, "I have nothing to put in it today" suggests writer's block. However, "purple" may be a sly reference to "purple prose," and therefore to a self-consciously poetic discourse. "Nothing" in the purple bucket results however in the completion of a poem.

"The Critic and the Poem" mocks the critic who survives best on a difficult poem, "a carcass / that will give him nourishment, that he can dissect." The word "carcass" allows the poet to turn on the image of a sheep's carcass, the death's head in his own poetry, as the poem moves from criticising the critic to criticising his own poetry:

> In Lewis I once saw
> a dead sheep on a moor. The crows had been at it.
> They had picked out its eyes like "green jewels"
> but more precisely I saw a mass of flies
> so thick about it I could hardly see the carcass.[55]

In *Consider The Lilies*, the flies pluck the eyes from a dead sheep "like gems from an old brooch" and in "Sunday Morning Walk" "the household air / was busy with buzzing like fever."[56] The simile from the novel belongs to a writer juxtaposing fine images and the monochromatic background of his homeland. The carcass of the sheep in "Sunday Morning Walk" halts a poetic response because the death's head lies outside his language, his perspective. I have shown how in *Love Poems and Elegies* perspective is suddenly and dramatically altered after the death of the poet's mother. The quotations show the poet using the conventions of print to pick out the luxurious simile "green jewels" from the text as precisely as the crows pluck out the eyes of the sheep because it no longer belongs to his discourse. The changed perspective adopted by the poet has made much redundant. "More precisely" marks his commitment towards a poetry which is not set apart or must be read in a certain way, but which is thrown into the world. The meanings of "carcass," "eyes" and "flies" are different from the meanings they had in "Sunday Morning Walk" because they take their place in a discourse of altered perspective which has recognised and absorbed the death's head. Here the poet is not discarding his language, as Crusoe did in an act of renunciation, but rather he has taken it up again to renegotiate it.

In The Middle establishes a language which is not new, but which yet is changed. It avoids commitment either to heaven or hell, either to the earlier poetry of epiphany or to the threatening raw flux. Identity is constantly negotiated, in the middle. In "The Scholar," the opening phrase "the scholar says" marks the persona as obsolete. His élitist isolation is threatened by nightmarish figures who invade his study. Crichton Smith suggested that MacDiarmid "was willing or was compelled to open himself out to life." The doubleness of that response is enacted here as the image of invaded isolation is balanced by a sense of excitement at the rewriting of the story in a new adult version:

> And I feel now it is the Day of the Wolf
> and not the Day of Little Red Riding Hood.
> The grannies are all being eaten in the wood.[57]

Inscribed in this changing text, the self seeks a new identity forged somewhere between the classic tragic hero and his modern counterpart, the Beckettian tramp. A precarious success is achieved:

> Sometimes I even forget who I once was
> and walk the road like a tramp, my face bristly,
> remembering vaguely my early crystal days.[58]

"Sometimes" does not completely destroy the memory of those other identities; "like" a tramp avoids vagrancy; "remembering vaguely" qualifies memory. Yet that phrase "my early crystal days" brings into the poem the earlier poet of the fine metaphor.

The Notebooks of Robinson Crusoe and *In The Middle* offer a self inscribed in time and place, and acknowledge that the I is not written but·read. The poem which gives *In The Middle* its title offers a disturbing image of confused identity and schizophrenic madness. The poet is caught between the world of scripture and Shakespeare, the sacred and the profane, Heaven and Hell. The poem asks "Who?," "What?," "Where?" and the question asked by "I" is met only by "Someone is painting the walls in a downpour of purple."[59] "In The Middle" offers a position at which a lost and fragmented self is vulnerable to the identity of a multiple of others.

"Someone," however, is part of a powerful new language. Time and place, those walls by which the self is formed, can be pushed out to form a space by a language which survives in the middle, avoiding commitment. The following lines appear purely referential, while suggesting endings, conclusion:

> Over the bare moor the late sun is shining,
> over the bristles of the lately cut corn.
> Somewhere in the distance a peewit's calling
> and a dog barks once from its iron chain.[60]

Yet the peewit's call and the dog's bark revitalise the scene. "Somewhere in the distance" avoids the definition of position; the single bark from a dog suggests the "iron chain" confines, yet does not silence. In these lines the poet finds images for a new poetry, acknowledging a barer, harder language, reaped through trial. The title of the poem itself, "Evening," not day, not night, occupies an expansive space and despite the anxiety expressed in the last stanza, and the apparent need to rehearse what will happen next, there is a proclamation of territory, a space created where the self will survive in the middle:

> Soon star after star will come out.
> Soon the moon will cast its eerie light
> over the weasel winding towards its prey
> and the fox grinning upward from its teeth.[61]

"Soon," "will come," "will cast" all defer the moment which defines. In that moment of deferral the poet lives, deferring death. The weasel who has not yet found his prey and the grinning fox means that the death's head exerts its influence: it is part of the perspective, included in the canvas of the poem, but does not silence the poet.

The Notebooks of Robinson Crusoe and *In The Middle* offer crisis poems, and a poet ruthlessly examining the very bases of his art, in an attempt to establish a starting point. It is through that crisis, and its survival, that he finds his community—a community of other writers. The title of "Those Who Move Others" suggests Shakespeare's sonnet, "They that have power to hurt, and will do none," but it is Dante who is celebrated in the first two lines quoted below:[62]

> If love that moves the stars
> and the spirals of dewy bouquets
> brings light to hunger
> then let the black grave
> with its tall mannerly worms
> welcome the silent minstrels.[63]

It is Dante who is kept in mind throughout this volume. If the interlocutor in the early poetry seemed to be the old woman in black, the Gaelic Matriarch, in this volume, more subtly, the interlocutor is Dante the literary patriarch. *The Divine Comedy* is the drama of the soul's choice between Heaven and Hell. The "I" of *In The Middle* moves between a heaven and a hell, too, attempting to find a position at which self can be fully inscribed. The title of the volume itself suggests the opening of *The Inferno*:

> In the midway of this our mortal life,
> I found me in a gloomy wood, astray,
> Gone from the path direct. . . .

The quotation above is the one used as an inscription in Crichton Smith's 1987 novel, *In The Middle of the Wood*, which explores the severe mental breakdown of its protagonist. Dante is kept in mind in the novel, too: Ralph Simmons experiences a night "infernal and terrible," a group therapy session is like one of the circles of *The Inferno*, and Ralph sees his duty in Dantean terms:

> Like Dante I must enter the final circle, he thought. I must burn there and find out about the fire and the mad shadows. That is what the Inferno is, the seethe of lost egos burning in their pain.[64]

Ralph draws back from that union with Dante. He finally understands tha "love was what moved the stars and the other planets and kept us steady in the stormy astronomy of reality."[65] The quotation absorbs the very last line of *The Paradiso* when Dante is silenced as his will and desire move in perfect harmony with God's love in an image of coincidence and wholeness, as self answers to God the father. Thus the first and last lines of Dante's poem constitute Crichton Smith's text of the novel and of *In The Middle*. Dante's journey is the poet's journey. Dante's trial is the poet's trial. The title, *The Divine Comedy*, would sit easily with Iain Crichton Smith's poems because the conjunction of the divine and comedy is something he explores here. In the eighteenth century, Dante was criticised for his lack of decorum because his language partook of several discourses; the sacred and the profane, the learned and the Latinised, provincial forms and dialect. That kind of variegated discourse is something Crichton Smith achieves, too.

Crichton Smith celebrates Dante because he too makes his own journey, and can finally celebrate a shared and whole identity in "we poets" because he has survived a similar potentially destructive crisis. This group is "a ring of cured poison," sharing a common fate:

> but we sing from thorns
> remembering the roses
> that shine at the bottom of wells.[66]

"Thorns," "roses," "wells," these are taken up again as the poet's discourse, part of the real world of his background, Lewis, yet the thorns, roses and wells of his poetry, too. In these lines, the poet gathers together the traditions of his own poetry. "Remembering" connects him with his poetic past and his background of Lewis, where no poetry was valued "unless it freely grows / in deep compulsion, like water in the well."[67] "Remembering" is repeated, acknowledging his connection not just with his own past, but with the great literary tradition begun with Homer, and Virgil and Dante. The protection of élitism has been drawn aside, yet claims can still be made for poetry:

> We send messages to each other
> in secret codes.
> In the invisible ink of our blood
> we walk down the neon streets
> of the same city.[68]

"Secret codes" offers a kind of underground community, not the "shared joke" and the language of exclusion of the poet of *From Bourgeois Land*. "Invisible ink of our blood" finds an image for language and an identity which inhabits both a literary tradition and modern flux, the "red" of the blood and the "yellow" of the street lamps offering up those characteristic colours of opposition. "The same city" offers the dispossessed community. It is a community of poets because, like him, each is a poem which is being written:

> and their ideas fly to them
> on accidental winds
> perching awhile in their minds
> from different valleys.[69]

The "I" discovers the community in whose discourse he is inscribed. It is a community unlike the poet's Lewis, which confined and defined:

symbolically he was son of the Calvinist matriarch. The community here does not define or confine, and he is inscribed, like them, as "stranger" and more importantly as "changing stranger."

To us, Homer, Virgil and Dante are created by and through their poetry: they are each effects of a text, "homo textual." The poet whose "I" is constructed in his lyrics recognises who he is now. Freed from the encompassing constructions of others, from his biography, the story of his life, he insists that the I is a poem, being written.

In The Middle explores ways of being in the middle. The title is also pertinent because it labels the key volume of an *oeuvre* which explores language and identity, holding together the language of the self-conscious early poet, and the poet of the later, barer verse, inhabiting fully neither identity, neither language. Midway between Heaven and Hell, and keeping both in mind. The death of his mother has presented the poet with the greatest challenge to his poetry-making and has demanded he confront the Lewis background. That confrontation is too dangerous, yet the protective and protected world of poetry has been irrevocably violated. In the middle describes where the self is inscribed. He survives as the outcast, the one who can never go home.

Notes

1. "Real People In A Real Place," in *Towards the Human* (Edinburgh: Macdonald, 1986), p. 27.
2. *The Notebooks of Robinson Crusoe* (London: Gollancz, 1975), Foreword.
3. *Ibid.*, p. 68.
4. *Ibid.*, p. 72.
5. *Ibid.*, p. 69.
6. *Ibid.*, p. 85.
7. "The Future of Gaelic Literature," *Transactions of the Gaelic Society of Inverness*, 43 (1961), 172-180 (p. 175).
8. *The Notebooks*, p. 85.
9. *Ibid.*
10. W. H. Auden, *The Enchafèd Flood* (London: Faber & Faber, 1951), pp. 97-98.
11. *The Notebooks*, p. 85.
12. *My Last Duchess* (London: Gollancz, 1971), p. 158.
13. Interview with Iain Crichton Smith, Taynuilt, 1987.
14. Carol Gow, "An Interview with Iain Crichton Smith," *Scottish Literary Journal*, 17:2 (November 1990), 43-57 (p. 47).
15. *The Notebooks*, p. 85.
16. Taynuilt Interview.
17. *New Poets* (London: Eyre & Spottiswoode, 1959), p. 18.
18. *The Notebooks*, p. 72.
19. *Ibid.*, p. 70.
20. Gerd Brand, *The Central Texts of Wittgenstein*, translated by Robert E. Innis (Oxford: Blackwell, 1979), p. 150.
21. W. H. Auden, *Secondary Worlds* (London: Faber, 1968), p. 222.
22. *The Notebooks*, p. 75.
23. *Goodbye Mr Dixon* (London: Gollancz, 1974), p. 72.

24. *The Notebooks*, p. 68.
25. *Ibid.*
26. "Between Sea and Moor," in *As I Remember*, edited by Maurice Lindsay (London: Hale, 1979), p. 108.
27. *The Notebooks*, p. 82; p. 83.
28. *Ibid.*, p. 73.
29. *Ibid.*, p. 89.
30. *Ibid.*
31. *Ibid.*
32. *Ibid.*, p. 90.
33. *Ibid.*, pp. 84-85.
34. *In The Middle Of The Wood* (London: Gollancz, 1987), p. 183.
35. *The Notebooks*, p. 87.
36. *Ibid.*
37. *Ibid.*, p. 30; p. 91.
38. *In The Middle*, p. 9.
39. *Ibid.*, p. 10.
40. *Ibid.*
41. *Ibid.*
42. Erich Auerbach, *Mimesis*, translated by Willard R. Trask (New Jersey: Princeton University Press, 1974), p. 8.
43. T. F. Merrill, "Sacred Parody and the Grammar of Devotion," *Criticism* (Winter 1981), 195-210.
44. *In The Middle*, p. 12.
45. *Ibid.*
46. *Ibid.*
47. Luke, 1.28-29.
48. *In The Middle*, p. 35.
49. *Ibid.*, p. 13.
50. "Hugh MacDiarmid: *Sangschaw* and *A Drunk Man Looks at the Thistle*," *Studies in Scottish Literature*, 7 (July, 1969-April 1970), 169-179 (p. 179).
51. *In The Middle*, p. 55.
52. *Ibid.*
53. "My Relationship With Poetry," *Chapman* 16, 4:4 (Summer 1976), 12-18 (p. 18).
54. William Wordsworth, Preface to *Lyrical Ballads*, edited by R. L. Brett and A. R. Jones (London: Methuen, 1971), p. 246.
55. *In The Middle*, p. 17.
56. *Consider the Lilies* (London: Gollancz, 1968), p. 99; "Sunday Morning Walk," *Thistles and Roses* (London: Eyre & Spottiswoode, 1961), p. 22.
57. *In The Middle*, p. 47.
58. *Ibid.*, p. 48.
59. *Ibid.*, p. 44.
60. *Ibid.*, p. 46.
61. *Ibid.*
62. William Shakespeare, *The Sonnets*, edited by John Dover Wilson (London: Cambridge University Press, 1966), p. 49.
63. *In The Middle*, p. 36.
64. *In The Middle of The Wood*, p. 47; p. 157.
65. *Ibid.*, p. 185.
66. *In The Middle*, p. 58.
67. *The Long River*, p. 16.
68. *In The Middle*, p. 58.
69. *Ibid.*, p. 64.

IV
Exile

CHAPTER SIX

Oedipus

Like Sophocles' Oedipus, the poet who has sought to forge his own identity has discovered that he is claimed by what is already written. His role has already been assigned: he has been born in a certain place at a certain time. The Oedipus legend taken up by Sophocles is an identity myth, a detective story which asks not whodunit but "who I am." Oedipus learns that he cannot write his own identity because it has already been written. The tragedy is sweet because it speaks of unity, salvation and community, but only at the cost of sacrificing Oedipus to his community. The drama operates on the oppositions of light and dark, blindness and sight, concealment and illumination, and the *méconnaisance*, the misrecognition and misnaming, of these. Only once these oppositions are examined does Oedipus *recognise* who he is. The destruction of Oedipus Rex signals the birth of the "I" who relinquishes the simplicity of neat opposition: the creation of his own history is interwoven with what is already assigned. He is husband *and* son, father *and* brother, redeemer *and* destroyer: identity is uncovered in contradiction. Pronouncing judgement, he inscribes himself under the sign of the curse, accepting blindness and banishment. The pestilence Oedipus brings with him is rampant individualism. The restoration of health is the claiming of the individual by his community because identity is inextricably bound up with community.

Oedipus, then, offers a useful figure in the narrative of Crichton Smith's own identity myth. The earlier constructions of Hamlet and Orpheus have allowed fruitful exploration of the Oedipus myth for a poet who has commented "one always feels the loss of a father."[1] Like Oedipus, the identity of the poet apparently free to choose identity in his poems is contradicted by his relationship with his community. Crichton Smith's comments on a poem by Donald MacAulay, "A Delicate Balance," illuminate a Sophoclean perception

123

of the relationship between community and individual. He sees MacAulay's poem as a narrative of sacrifice and redemption, dealing with

> the negative side of the community . . . which will not allow for the particularities of the individual. The person in this poem is a sacrifice to the community, he represents the human cost of keeping the community in balance, he is the scapegoat which keeps the community healthy.[2]

The movement of Crichton Smith's poetry has been away from restricting inscription, away from his Gaelic inheritance, away from a Scottish stereotyped myth, in a process of individualisation. The poems of *The Notebooks* established him as outcast, but the discovery made was that, like Oedipus, identity is uncovered, discovered, in contradiction: the self is written *and* read in the mirror of his community. The narrative I have offered, therefore, must culminate not in a cosy story of homecoming, but with the choice of eternal homelessness, the precarious position of dislocation and disjunction.

The title of the opening poem in *The Exiles*, "Returning Exile," is a rich one. It names the poet who comes back to publishing poetry after a long absence: there is a significant gap of seven years between publication of *In The Middle* and the subsequent *The Exiles* in 1984. Crichton Smith suffered a mental breakdown in 1982. For a long period he thought he would never write again, a black period during which he was effectively exiled from any identity he had created for himself. There is no body of poetry to fill the lacuna in the narrative: though he wrote poetry during this time he was dissatisfied with much of it and consequently published no new collections. Crichton Smith's poetry has always been distinctive because of its continual reworking and redefining of themes in an increasingly complex examination of the bases of his art, an exploration where territory is claimed slowly and in public. Yet *The Exiles* stands apart from the preceding volumes not just because of these seven years but because of its silence about these seven years. Returning from the wilderness, he has gained terrible knowledge. In a new hard and spare verse, he exposes the misnaming of experience: of exile, of heroes, of tragedy. And in "A Life" he traces an Oedipal narrative of freedom, punishment and redemption.

"Returning Exile" opens a collection where the silence about the poet's past is prescribed in the negative injunction of the opening lines, "You who come home do not tell me / anything about yourself."[3] These lines offer a text which constructs identity; "you" and "me" pivot on the word "home." The experiences of the returning exile, the stories he can tell about himself, his history, are not to be told, as the "where" and the "why" of that other self are denied. In the last stanza, the injunction "do not tell" is repeated and the "you" is named by the speaker as "beloved stranger":

> Do not tell me where you have come from, beloved stranger.
> It is enough that there is light still in your eyes,
> that the dog rising on his pillar of black knows you.[4]

The silence is prescribed by the community. To tell is to take responsibility for the creation of self. Here that creativity is negated. "Beloved" pulls towards an identity, towards an inscription of beloved son, but "stranger" frees itself from the position. There is a seductive sense of homecoming here: the poet has returned from the dead, he has returned from the Inferno of madness. Yet though he returns, he is not claimed here. "It is enough" marks a different kind of relationship: less obsessive, more relaxed, more expansive. "Home" here is read as a physical space, a community, but "home" is also poetry itself, and a poet who finds a space in which to write, who accepts the silence of those seven years and yet who finds a new and rich productivity: "it is enough."

Accepting the gap, the lacuna, the poet does not attempt to write across it. The history, the individual's place within his community, is a text of conflict, of life and death. That conflict can never be resolved. Crichton Smith's short story, "Chagall's Return," accepts the same interconnection and the same irreconcilability:

> I feel sticky stuff on my clothes, my hands and my face. I carry the village with me, stamped all over my body, and take it with me, roof, door, bird, branch, pails of water. I cross the Atlantic with it.
> "Welcome," they say, "but what have you got there?"
> "It is a nest," I say, "and a coffin."
> "Or, to put it another way, a coffin and a nest."[5]

The nest which offers home, life and identity, also offers death. Such a conflict has led the poet into the Inferno of madness. To choose dislocation is to find a way to exist within that conflict.

"Speech for a Woman" is also a speech for Scotland, and a people whom "history has condemned . . . to departure."[6] When her children leave, and the woman asks "where?" they in their youth can answer "everywhere." Against the outlook of her single window they offer the challenge of a landscape of colour; "blue," "blackens," "brown," "green" and a changing landscape of "seas" and "desert": against her immobility they offer travel; "ships," "trains," "buses": against her isolation they offer the universal conditions of war and famine. "Everywhere" is a world of colour, travel, war and hunger. The poem closes with the image of the sandglass bringing time and decay as, her children gone, the woman is released from her identity

125

as mother into a strange liberation. Nest and coffin describe that universal movement away which teaches only return, and that in the beginning is the end. To be content to exist within that contradiction and collision, without attempting to re-write the script, is to find a new basis for his art, life-giving and fruitful. The poet who turns to the theme of exile is aware of the dangers of misnaming the home and examines therefore not just one of the universal themes of literature, but his own history, his own fragmentation and fracture, his own story, exploring the concept of home, and insisting on the duality, the nest and the coffin.

Scotland's literature is permeated with poems and songs about exile. "Speech For A Woman" shows a changed and changing Gaeldom, in contrast to a literature which is frequently guilty of looking back to a homeland which, if it ever existed, is not allowed to change. Crichton Smith has drawn comparison between the "facile ceilidh" and the poem: the former is "an attempt to freeze experience," the latter "a real living study of the effects exile can have on highly gifted individuals."[7] Misnaming the home is an understandable, but dangerous, impulse:

> One feels compelled to name it, and sometimes to do so falsely. The fact of the exile leads to the lie which is intended to comfort and to fix the home.[8]

In the image of the sandglass, therefore, is the antithesis to the "freezing" of experience, bringing both liberation and loss.

"When They Reached The New Land" reveals how a sense of home can be achieved, not by calling "new mountains by old names," but by accepting the foreignness. "Naming" here leads only to a sense of misfit:

> Nevertheless there was a sort of slantness,
>
> a curious odd feeling in the twilight
> that the mountain had shifted, had cast off its name.[9]

"Shifted" and "cast off its name" are positive achievements because ultimately the act of naming is the act of misnaming, of freezing experience. The poet's experiences of growing up on Lewis as a bilinguist, his explorations as a writer, have taught him only the mismatch between language and the world with which we try to master it. "A curious odd feeling in the twilight" marks uncertainty, uneasiness and opens up possibility. It is in awareness of this mismatch that a truth is eventually found: "And they were at peace / among their settled, naturalised names."

Yet such a gradual working out of a relationship is denied the immigrant in "There Is No Sorrow," where the land is described in terms of a text which the exile cannot read. His "dumb grief" stems from being set down among "strange names," "new rocks." "Shadows," "tales," "sky" and "stars" offer an unintelligible text. Home is seen in a wavering, dream-like image because, seen in the stars which are "not the same," it is misnamed. The world before him is created in a childlike or Whitmanesque list:

> But the strange names stand up against him
> and the dryness of the earth
> and the cold barks of dogs
> and his sails are folded in this harbour
> which is not his.[10]

The repetitive "and" enacts the sterility of this situation which piles up barren, negative experiences to which the exile cannot respond. The sails which carried the exiles from their islands to find new homes are "folded in this harbour" but "folded" and the last line quoted above chillingly dismiss any sense of home and haven implied in the word "harbour." This exile is luckier than Robinson Crusoe, however, because he has a narrator. It is the poet who names here, who can identify both the fact and the lie, and describe the "poor lost exile" caught between the two. The line "for you there is nothing but endurance" pushes the exile away from the poet. The "dumb" exile cannot speak his part and must rely on a *Deus Ex Machina* solution:

> till one miraculous day
> you will wake up in the morning
> and put on your foreign clothes
> and know that they are at last yours.[11]

The poem enacts transit: the clothes cease to be foreign on the enjambment. Yet it is significant that this transition occurs in a gap in the exile's narrative: like the poet's own narrative, there is a lacuna in the story.

For the emigrants, Canada and Australia were the new lands which beckoned with promise. In "Australia," a group of four poems, the poet uses explicitly images of fabulation. These emigrants have "surrendered to its legend" and have found a new home. The Scotland they have freed themselves from is a land of "graves sanctified by God" and "historical darknesses," the land they have travelled to offers "a music being continually reborn." Both Scotland and Australia can claim the individual who lives there but the new land has a future, and not just a past. Dislocation means carrying with you those graves and the historical darknesses. It is a curious half-freedom, and home is half loved, half hated, the nest and the grave.

Such dislocation means never surrendering to the legend. For

Crichton Smith the legend in its widest sense is the way language orders the world, makes it safe and known, and enables the individual to feel at home. The legend also suggests the story the poet has written for himself in his poetry. His own legend, his own language, is criticised, scrutinised, elucidated, and truth is found where misnaming is uncovered. The death of his mother pointed out the misnaming in his own poetry which refused the contradictions of identity.

A comment Crichton Smith made in 1980 after a visit to Australia suggests that history, the past, is now part of his canvas. It is limiting, dangerous, yet highly prized:

> It is possible that a country has to be lived in for a long time before it can develop the history and the shadow and the contradictions that are necessary for great literature.[12]

All literature is made up of words, yet the distinction drawn is one between a literature which is simply text, and a literature in which text is linked to a history: that history brings shadow and contradiction, which in many ways is textuality's antithesis, yet it is precisely that tension Crichton Smith now seeks in his own work.

His own heroes offered him a script in a private tragedy. Opening up his own myth to the world, the tragic hero found a place in a public comedy of existence. In this collection, the poet contemplates a photograph of Ned Kelly, an "iron mask in his iron armour." The legend of Ned Kelly provides a fixed identity, a written and closed script:

> However dingos leap at it they will not chew him
> for he is a story, a poem,
> a tale that is heard on the wind.[13]

Like the skins of Hamlet and Orpheus which protected and sustained, this iron skin is exposed as a "shabby skin." In the poem, Ned Kelly is legend and photograph. The photograph captures only a frozen moment of time; the legend does not allow death to be written into the script. The insistent use of "iron" in the poem and the lines "stiffly in the wind / which blew past the ravens" suggest the rigidity of identity, the absence of darkness, contradiction—and death. "In that dry land his armour will not rust" incorporates, by its very absence, the sea. In Crichton Smith's work, the epithet "salt" often carries the whole weight of his Gaelic inheritance which breaks in on his legend of identity: an inheritance of his own history which brings loss and liberation.

Other great legends are liberated, too. Odysseus and Prince Charles are offered new scripts. The title of his poem about Odysseus, which does not name him, "Next Time," and the opening injunction,

"Listen," foreground the plasticity of an identity created anew at each time of telling. Crichton Smith's Odysseus overlays all the other identities, the other "shabby skins" of this hero. Against the freedom that comes with fabulation are set limitations: "salt bronzed veteran" employs the image of the salt sea and the association of its antithesis to textuality; Odysseus is urged to listen to his past, a past represented by metaphors of death as "cries of the dead / haunt the gaunt headland," the internal rhyme suggesting an echoing, repetitive history.[14] Crichton Smith suggests a re-scripting of this legend of the hero who comes home to a country and finds it all fits. Here there is "no return" because Odysseus the wanderer can never come home. He, and home, will have changed. Even though he returns, he will bring with him his own separate past of the Trojan war. Crichton Smith offers a new ending:

> Next time, do this,
> salt bronzed veteran
> let the tapestry be unfinished
> as truthful fiction is.[15]

To "let the tapestry be unfinished" is to refuse the ending of homecoming. "Truthful fiction" demands that Odysseus is stripped of his script of the tragic hero. The precarious balancing act that is achieved identity is enacted in this poem as "never surrendering to the legend" and allows the poet to rename the king as exile, but slyly defer the act of naming until "Next time."

Prince Charles Edward Stuart is treated less well. The standard English of the title, "Prince Charles," immediately and effectively exiles Bonnie Prince Charlie from his cultural identity, his own legend of Romantic hero denied his birthright. Charlie's naivety is revealed in his desire "to stamp," to write his identity on this land, as Crusoe once wished to write his identity on a desert island: "a fresh land to put his stamp on. / This was in the end his hoped-for home."[16] Such a script ignores history, community, and succumbs to the temptation of perceiving individuality in isolation, unconnected to community. Like Crichton Smith's heroes, Prince Charles discovers that the individual and community are irrevocably interlinked. The nature he intended to put his stamp on blurs his identity as "The dizzying snow blossomed against his face." Prince Charles turns away, "his torn shirt a tail, the sun so warm / and still adventurous on his secret boat." Turning from the snow to the sun and the "secret boat" suggests a new island of self, a retreat from the crisis of identity. Departure is a positive position in Crichton Smith's work. It is arrival that traps, and in Italy, Charles "fattened steadily far from that gaunt waste." In a line which neatly juxtaposes the oppositions of plenty and paucity Crichton Smith brings into his poem the conflict that will keep his own poetry on the path he has chosen: a path in which the myth of identity is tethered, controlled and perhaps even judged by "that gaunt waste" of his inheritance. Charles, however, has failed to engage with contradiction, and has grown bloated by his own legend in an Italy of sun and wine. In Crichton Smith's poem, Charles is a weak drunkard.

"To put his stamp on" is a metaphor of the writing of identity. The white snow which obliterates the romantic figure is an image which denies writing and offers an image of blankness. The metaphor of writing and its opposite, blankness, is foregrounded in *The Notebooks* but it is part of the texture of Crichton Smith's work. His comments on his own background offer illumination of the basis of the metaphor. Individualism and community are seen as incompatible: "I have forsaken the community in order to individualise myself."[17] The comment is a curiously dramatic, heightened one, perhaps because it lies behind the impulse which creates the identities in his poetry. It is not unusual, perhaps, for a poet to feel at odds with his background, but for Crichton Smith the individualisation is very much tied in with his English poetry, and a created self which placed him outside his community, among "the artists, the guilty and gifted ones."[18] To "forsake" is a betrayal: "guilty and gifted" are the twin crimes of the individual who, like Oedipus, stands outside the community and threatens its structure. To write in English, and not Gaelic, is seen as an act of hostility, "almost to be a traitor."[19]

The conflict of factors which afforded Crichton Smith a new language at five years old made him realise early that the conflict between Gaelic and English was not only a linguistic dilemma but a social and political one.[20] The adult writer who contemplates his two languages of Gaelic and English continues to see the choice as a social and political one. Not to uphold the Gaelic culture when it is threatened with extinction may seem traitorous to the many people and organisations which try to defend and uphold it, but Crichton Smith's stance on the question of Gaelic is complex: he is distressed by the possible loss of one language among many, yet reluctant to interfere with a natural free course. This study of Crichton Smith's poetry has traced the myth of identity in the English poetry. However, it is pertinent here to remind the reader of Crichton Smith's standing as a Gaelic writer. He has enriched Gaelic literature to such an extent that the epithet "traitor" can hardly apply. Yet by writing in English, indeed by offering translations of Gaelic poems, does he thereby deny Gaelic culture the considerable support and prestige he could bring to it if he could be claimed as a Gaelic writer like, for example, Sorley MacLean? Although I have maintained that the choice of language was in fact made for him, there is no doubt that the tension between Gaelic and English is an important one and can usefully be explored here with reference to Gaelic poetry available in translation by Crichton Smith himself.

Crichton Smith's contribution to Gaelic literature includes poems, prose, and drama. He has also written several children's books, ranging from *Little Red Riding Hood and An Dorus Iarùinn* [The Iron Door], a brightly illustrated story book for younger children, to *Iain am Measg Nan Reultan* [Iain Among The Stars], a space fantasy for older children. If Gaelic survives, it can only survive as a living, spoken language, a language spoken by the young in their own environment. If Crichton Smith's books for children written in Gaelic encourage this, they will fill a gap he sensed in his own youth. One of the reasons it seemed natural for him to write in English was that there were no books in Gaelic equivalent to *Treasure Island* or the books of P. C. Wren.[21] Crichton Smith does not gloss over the difficulties of the survival of Gaelic:

> I think in English. I feel much easier speaking in English than in Gaelic and so I think do most Gaelic speakers, except the old. This has something to do with the fact that Gaelic vocabulary for the things that I'm interested in hardly exists. For instance it would be extremely difficult to write a book of literary criticism in Gaelic. A whole new vocabulary would have to be created.[22]

This admission reveals why Crichton Smith's attitude to Gaelic is often ambivalent and why he has never written in patriotic terms about Gaelic. He is, however, strongly interested in the preservation of Gaelic as one language among many, as one way of looking at the world, one way of creating that world.

Such a stance seems to many Gaelic activists dangerously careless. There is no doubt that despite a much-publicised revival in interest in Gaelic, the language is in a fragile state. Derick Thomson argues for positive action to preserve and invigorate the language. In his book *Why Gaelic Matters* he warns that while statistics seem to indicate that the Gaelic population has stabilised and that there has been an improvement in literacy, the level of Gaelic usage among the young gives cause for concern. He points out that the language has also suffered interference from the English language system.[23] Crichton Smith has remarked that when he visits Lewis and speaks to the children he meets in Gaelic, they will answer him in English. The young Gael, perhaps, like the young Scot, is pressured by the media to see the Gaelic language, and the Scots dialect, as inferior to English, and those who speak these languages as inferior. Television has been instrumental in exacerbating the problem, changing island life.

In "Return to Lewis," Crichton Smith explores this encroachment of a foreign culture and writes of "English growing as the Gaelic dies" yet his tongue is firmly placed in cheek here:

> Ah, those eves
> of fine September moons and autumn sheaves
> when no-one knocked on doors, and fish was free,
> before the Bible faded to TV.[24]

The ambivalent response reveals "Those eves" as part of a past that cannot be retrieved. While Derick Thomson is firmly committed to preserving the Gaelic language, Crichton Smith is perhaps nervous of this and the lines quoted above enact the danger: preserving a dead culture freezes and distorts it. While Derick Thomson is keen to see all-Gaelic schools, and feels that the inroads that have been made towards bilingualism do not go far enough, castigating "faint-hearted" education officials and councillors who cannot or will not counter lack of parental and public confidence, Crichton Smith's background would make him unsympathetic towards such power wielded over the young. He explores language and world in the sequence "Am Faigh A' Ghàidhlig Bàs?" which he has also translated into English, an act which in itself reveals Crichton Smith's stance here.

The title of the sequence "Am Faigh A' Ghàidhlig Bàs?" [Shall Gaelic Die?] is a Gaelic cliché, an ironical title referring to what Highlanders say in patriotic terms about their language.[25] There are twenty-five poems in the sequence and I refer to the translation by Crichton Smith in *Selected Poems 1955-1980*. The fifth in the sequence proposes:

> He who loses his language loses his world. The Highlander who loses his language loses his world.
> The space ship that goes astray among planets loses the world.[26]

Crichton Smith acknowledges that Gaelic is more than a language—it is a way of life. Citing MacDiarmid's "yow-trummle," he says this description of winter, when the sheep tremble with cold, reveals a people and their world. All language does this, he insists.[27] When a language dies, a way of life dies, too: "Shall Gaelic die! What that means is: shall we die?"

But if language frames a world, that frame is also a prison:

> Were you ever in a maze? Its language fits your language. Its roads fit the roads of your head. If you cannot get out of the language you cannot get out of the maze. Its roads reflect your language. O for a higher language, like a hawk in the sky, that can see the roads, that can see their end, like God who built the roads, our General Wade. The roads of the Highlands fit the roads of our language.[28]

For Crichton Smith, poetry itself promises a higher language, a way to get out of the maze. If that is an impossible dream, then many languages allow at least for a diversity:

> A million colours are better than one colour, if they are different.
> A million men are better than one man if they are different.
> Keep out of the factory, O man, you are not a robot. It wasn't a factory that made your language—it made you.[29]

And in the juxtaposition of the image of the rainbow and mist, Crichton Smith argues for diversity and heterogeneity:

> Like a rainbow, like crayons, spectrum of beautiful languages. The one-language descended like a church—like a blanket, like mist.[30]

Gaelic, then, is one of many languages and thus valued. Yet if it is to be of value, it must survive as a spoken language, changing the world and being changed by the world. Crichton Smith's desire to see Gaelic survive, therefore, is countered by a disinclination to stop its free, natural course, to attempt to freeze it. It is therefore a course which could lead to its disintegration and destruction. This mutability is explored in:

> I came with a "sobhrach" in my mouth. He came with a "primrose."
> A "primrose by the river's brim." Between the two languages, the word "sobhrach" turned to "primrose."
> Behind the two words, a Roman said "prima rosa."
> The "sobhrach" or the "primrose" was in our hands. Its reasons belonged to us.[31]

To lose a language, then, is to be impoverished: if Gaelic dies, "Scotland will be weakened more than it suspects, more than it will ever know."[32]

"A Meditation on Gaelic" is a long poem in 53 sections, written in English in three-line stanzas. Here there is a confidence that a language can never die:

> Nothing dies, not even a language dies.
> Though we should cease to speak it, it doesn't die.
> It is retained in our old manuscripts,
>
> and somehow through our bones it still shines,
> evidence of humanity and love.[33]

Yet "retained in our old manuscripts" depicts a language no longer living on the tongue. This "treasury of exile and of stones" is part of a history.

If Crichton Smith is reluctant to impose the speaking of Gaelic on young Gaels, he nevertheless has been instrumental in nurturing the language through his writing. The fragility of the language means that developing the language so that it can survive in the twentieth century must be done cautiously. Crichton Smith's poem, "You are at the bottom of my mind," reveals how he has been able to extend the subject matter of Gaelic poetry without ignoring the rich Gaelic tradition. Here he combines traditional Gaelic imagery of the sea to describe psychological state:

> And you will never rise to the surface of the sea, even though my hands should be ceaselessly hauling, and I do not know your way at all, you in the half-light of your sleep, haunting the bottom of the sea without ceasing, and I hauling and hauling on the surface of the ocean.[34]

Yet if to have two languages is to be enriched, "how shall the single poem come out true / in this slant feeling, slant geography?" The poet who attempts to forge a whole identity for himself in his English poems sees himself, as Gael, destined to stand for ever at the crossroads:

> foreigners in the evening, in the rain,
> lost in the mist, always standing at crossroads,
> for history to tell us what we are.[35]

Or to be dressed in "the dress of the fool, the two colours that have tormented me—English and Gaelic."

To accept the label "guilty and gifted" therefore denies the stature of Crichton Smith as a Gaelic writer, and denies the way he has enriched and developed the language. Nevertheless, the constant restructuring of identity I trace in his English poetry reveals a desire to confront fragmentation, to unite the story with the history. To be "guilty and gifted" is in part to write in English, certainly, but perhaps more important than the conflict between Gaelic and English in his English poetry is the conflict between a language constructed of abstracts and brilliant metaphor, and a harder, barer verse which attempts a "Calvinistic honesty," and embraces his history.

If Crichton Smith's poetry was changed after his mother's death, it is significant that his identification of home and dislocation turns on death, too. Those who leave are also named by the phrase which names those who stay: "where they have not disowned their dead."[36] In rewriting the legend of Odysseus, the poet demanded that Odysseus's return included the history of the dead of the Trojan War. The death of his mother broke in on Crichton Smith's script. Several poems enact that violation.

The image of a language breaking in and causing a disruption which is also a setting free occurs in "Speech For A Woman" and in "You'll

Take A Bath." In "Speech For A Woman," the frost which carves an unintelligible language on the single window is the frost in which her children imprint their own footsteps. In "You'll Take A Bath," a poem about the poet's relationship with his mother, graffiti are the language which breaks in on the literary constructions the poet has woven around the relationship. Mother and son are seen as damsel in the tower and knight of chivalric romance, yet the description of the council scheme where "each flower / in the grudging garden died in trampled clay" belies that construction and an image of writing breaking in exposes the misnaming:

> At the second turning of the stony stair
> the graffiti were black letters in a book
> misspelt and menacing.[37]

The first line, echoing T. S. Eliot's "At the second turning of the second stair" from "Ash Wednesday, 1930," offers the kind of page in which self wishes to be inscribed: English literature, English poetry. Yet violating that sacred page are graffiti. Such violation, however, is liberating, offering him something which seems real and contemporary. Crichton Smith has linked graffiti with a "reality" which lies behind the appearance of society:

> Graffiti . . . shows the aggression of the "homeless," the language of hatred, ferocious and misspelt . . . the grotesque language which is the reality that lies deeply beneath the contradictions of schools and other institutions.[38]

The "homeless" one in his own poetry, the individual raised on Lewis, the man of flesh and blood, demands to be written, too, to find a part on the page to record his presence. The poet in the last stanza who visits his mother's grave admits "I feel the sweat / stink my fresh shirt out." Symbolically the fresh shirt represents the identity of a man untainted by his past. The "bath" is the pretext by which his mother detains him and also another cleansing of self from the relationship as he leaves. Such division cannot be maintained, and "sweat," the "sticky stuff" that clings to Chagall's clothes, hands and face, reverses the cleansing in an act of baptism which names him son. Her death, the apparent ultimate liberation, does not free him:

> And almost I am clean but for that door
> so blank and strong, imprinted with her name
> as that far other in the scheme was once,
> and "scheme" becomes a mockery, and a shame,
> in this neat place, where each vase has its flower,
> and the arching willow its maternal stance.[39]

A clean getaway is impossible. Death has separated them, but he, like the door and the gravestone, is "imprinted with her name." The image of the vase in Crichton Smith's early work was an image of perfection in which opposition and contradiction were contained. In the quotation above, the vase is part of the landscape of the poem, not just a metaphor, and thus reflects on his early solutions in the same way that this neat landscape of the dead reflects on the housing "scheme" of the living.

The elegies Crichton Smith wrote for his mother after her death are marked by language which denies the solutions of his early poetry and by the crisis of threatened silence. Here the reverberation of the word "vase" shows a poet finding new ways to use his language. He is still suspicious of metaphor but however much he negates it the earlier image is allowed to break through. The poet's own past, the language of his poetry, was steadily relinquished in an act of dispossession, but the movement in this volume is reversed: he re-establishes a connection with his past, his language. The word "vase" does not surrender to the legend, to Crichton Smith's poetic construction, but neither is that construction negated.

Metaphor of the early kind, however, is rare. The reasons, perhaps, can be explained by Crichton Smith's comments on the early poem, "For My Mother":

> It is easy for me to write a poem saying that the blood which I shed in my poetry is like the blood which ran from her gloves on those cold foreign mornings and in that salty light; but that is not sufficient, for it is not an aesthetic fact, nor can it be resolved aesthetically, that one should have to leave home at such an age to do a job like the gutting of herring so far from one's own home.
>
> For these reasons I have been always suspicious of the glitteringly aesthetic. Metaphor can sometimes be used to conceal insoluble contradictions in life, and Yeats's poem, "Easter 1916," did not solve the Irish crisis, it only clarified it. In the end, society lives and works outside the metaphor, and to think that the metaphor solves anything except the problems set by the poet would be silly and unrealistic. Beyond the poems of Seamus Heaney, beautiful though they are, the masked men will stand above the draped coffins saluting an empty heaven with their guns.[40]

Art and life are separated here—and more specifically, poetry and death. "You'll Take A Bath" clarifies the contradiction between a "real"environment and the poetic, literary construction which does not master it, between a "real" relationship and the attempt to record it in poetry. Seamus Heaney offers here agreement with Crichton Smith's point of view, but is apparently happy to discuss art and life as separate entities:

Art is an image. It is not a solution to reality, and to confuse the pacifications and appeasements and peace of art with something that is attainable in life is a great error. But to deny your life the suasion of art-peace is also an unnecessary Puritanism.[41]

"An unnecessary Puritanism" is Crichton Smith's "Calvinistic honesty," and the quality he has deliberately embraced. His suspicion of metaphor is explained in a text about death and the poem which explores the disjunction between art and life revolves around his mother's death. The death's head is always a threat to the poet—threatening silence.

"Speech for Prospero" is for the Prospero of *The Tempest*, for the Prospero of Auden's "The Sea and The Mirror," and it is also for the Prospero-like early figure who has made a conscious decision to abandon a dandyish language, who has become disenchanted with metaphor. Yet significantly this new identity is deferred till the future, and Prospero's speech is made when he is neither home nor away, but at the point of departure, "Music working itself out in the absurd halls and the mirrors" describes the relationship between poetry and life, metaphor and society, but the relationship and the commitment is deferred. The position of dislocation and disjunction is a position taken up in language itself.

Such a position brings both isolation and liberation. In "For Poets Writing in English Over In Ireland," Crichton Smith explores not just the conflict of Gaelic and English but the conflict of identity that comes with the language. The poem is a complex one of islands, doors, rooms and worlds, words connected with identity in this poet's work. Significantly, he is an outsider here: he sits "outside the room / where a song in Irish walzed the Irish round."[42] The group of Irish poets are "they" to his "I." He is outside the conversation, too, constantly drawn to the sense of Irishness around him, which these poets do not seem to notice. The poets writing in English are an island in that Irishness to which the writer is delivered not just because they converse in English but because their subject matter is poetry. Yet they are only an island because the poet here is constantly aware of the Irishness which surrounds them. Comparing poets Dunn and Larkin, the group decides

> "Now Dunn is open
> to more of the world than aging Larkin is.
>
> What room was Mr Bleaney in? It's like
> going to any tenement and finding
> any name you can think of on the door.
>
> And you wonder a little about him but not much."[43]

Their judgement seems to accord with Crichton Smith's own ideas about a poetry which admits the fact world but does not succumb to its ordinariness. The image of the tenement door and "any name you can think of" recalls "You'll Take A Bath" and the identity of a poet for whom "any name you can think of" is limited by something already written.

The metaphors "To enter a different room" and "I turn a page" allow the outsider to contemplate other positions: "To enter a different room. When did Bleaney / dance to the bones? This world is another world."[44] "Dance" and "bones" suggest poetry and death, and turn on the relationship of metaphor and society. To dance to the bones suggests a poet of extremity and passion, a poetry surviving the confrontation with the death's head.

Contrasting Yeats's poetry with the poetry of an unnamed poet, the poet here returns to the image of the door to name Yeats international and unique: "his international name was on the door / and who would ask who had been there before him?"[45] Yeats, "creator of yourself, a conscious lord" argued for the Mask, a "phantasmagoria," and for the poet as type, as Lear, Romeo, Oedipus, Tiresias.[46] Yeats offers a wholeness different from the fragmentation of the man. Crichton Smith, too, once demanded such wholeness. The unnamed poet who writes of the death of his wife in Irish Gaelic offers a private poetry in comparison to Yeats's public voice. While Yeats wrote in English, the unnamed poet writes in Irish Gaelic. Choosing their poetry, their language, they choose identity.

In a return to the three poets of his group, Crichton Smith sees himself:

> They are me,
> poised between two languages. They have chosen
> with youth's superb confidence and decision.[47]

Yet they "have chosen," while he remains "poised." And while their choice is between Irish Gaelic and English, it is not simply the choice between Scots Gaelic and English that concerns the poet here but a much more complex choice between a poetry in English and a poetry in Gaelic, between the persona which like that of Yeats is divorced from the accidence of the man, and the persona like that of the unnamed poet who writes of his own wife's death. Again the choices collapse into choices of identity. "Poised" means he has not chosen, and the last lines of the poem rewrite the quotation of the Irish poem in metaphors of fracture and division:

> "Half of my side you were, half of my seeing,
> half of my walking you were, half of my hearing."
> Half of this world I am, half of this dancing.[48]

The Irish poet writes of loss on the death of his wife. It was another death, the death of Crichton Smith's mother, which fractured identity for the poet. Yet, here, he can write of gain. To be inscribed fully neither in the language of "society" nor metaphor, to find identity neither in a created script, nor the script handed to him by his culture, is to find truth and freedom in division, to celebrate disjunction.

When Crichton Smith writes of "The Survivors" or "The 'Ordinary' People," it may look as if he has abandoned gods and heroes of literature. Yet words connected with textuality continually break through. "The Survivors" "whose days do not form a book" are different from him because he spends his days working to produce the physical object of a book. Yet the poet's days also form a book because the poet *is* a book, a collection of poems which form the days in which his identity is formed whole, in Yeats's phrase, "something intended, complete." The poem turns on incompletion and completion, completion linked not just with wholeness but with art. "Admire them most of all," those for whom the part is sufficient: "The hyphens, the dashes, the strokes—" are the textual marks which name them, forever deferring completion of the text, and thus a wholeness which would freeze that text. Yet the poet here inscribes these survivors as Sisyphus: "they push stones away from their breasts / when they rise in the morning."[49] In "The 'Ordinary' People," too, an insistent literariness breaks through as the poet contemplates those who "live precariously by the deaths of roses, / and hang their washing among tragedies."[50] To place "washing" alongside "tragedies" is not just a mixing of concrete and abstract, characteristic of Crichton Smith's work, but gives "tragedies" a new setting amongst the domestic, just as it places a word from the lexicon of literature into a text of everyday. The last stanza wedges a division between "tragedies" and "tragedy"; the first belongs to the world, the second to the theatre, a falsely protected text which deceives and offers instead of a hero a "red infant / howling and screaming from his wooden cage."[51] The poet who achieves such insight occupies a complicated position of division, yet, "Who Daily" celebrates fragmentation: he is "Venus with the one arm, / Apollo with the one leg."[52] The "who" of the poem is not named, and insists that identity is forged each day in writing, finding in incompleteness, fragmentation and plasticity, an identity.

Yet if the poet finds a truth in never surrendering to the legend, in avoiding commitment and definition, there are others who will attempt to define and confine him. "The Legend" offers a schoolfriend's memories of "what seemingly I was," "the anthology of memories of the other." Yet that definition is welcomed, too, as identity after identity is overlaid so that perhaps in that complex a truth is found:

> My fear
> or rather hope is that I am put back
> further and further in that clutch of tales
> till I am lost for ever to these fables,
>
> O false and lying and yet perhaps true.[53]

"Fear" and "hope" are interchangeable because there is an ambiguity to the lines above which centres on another pair of oppositions, "clutch" and "lost." The "clutch of tales" suggests an identity formed within his society. "These fables" may refer to "clutch of tales" or to the scripts he has created in opposition. "To be lost for ever" may express the desire to be fully at home within his Gaelic society, and thus to be "lost" to the other identities, or it may welcome these memories as another identity, another script to overlay his own. The ambiguity is continued with the interchangeability of the oppositions of falsehood and truth, and the last five lines offer no resolution because meaning hinges on the ambiguity of the construction of the verb:

> I would be barer with no foliage round me,
> without a title, a great blank behind me,
>
> and only a real future ahead,
> myself with a caseful of impersonal poems,
> unsalted, bare, and floating out of my arms.[54]

Is "I would be" conditional, or does it express desire? Does it warn that such freedom would result in a blank script, and no identity, or does it desire to cut free from the past? Does "a real future ahead" deliver the self to the limitations of the real, fact world, or does it offer freedom from a restricting past? Which identity is "myself"? And does the description of the poems as "unsalted" offer a good or bad poetry? Answers to these questions are denied within the canvas of the poem, and the poet remains poised between two meanings, at the point of departure.

"Envoi," the poem which closes the collection, proclaims new territory. It offers points of departure, poise, images of limitation lightened by the promise of freedom, images of freedom weighted by memories of limitation. "Bones" and "roses" are words from the lexicon of *Thistles and Roses*, a lexicon of contraries where a black Calvinism was contrasted with images of colour, life and freedom. Here, the poet breaks free of that rigid polarity. "Windows" and "doors" enclose and confine but also now provide entry on to the world, and the sea, sometimes an image of Calvinism, sometimes an image of freedom, is now both at the same time.

> Consider
> how the sea roars mournfully at the edge of
> all things, how the seaweed
> hangs at the sailor's neck, the crab
> shuffles in armour.[55]

The positioning of "at the edge of" at the line end and "hangs" at the beginning of the line wedges open a space between an image of freedom and its limitation. The injunction "consider" leaves this knowledge suspended, neither rejected nor accepted. And a similar space is found by the speaker who is a Hamlet, but who denies tragedy:

> Tragedy is
> nothing but churned foam.
> I wave to you
> from this secure and leafy entrance,
> this wooden
> door on which I bump my head,
> this moment and then,
> that.[56]

Again, a wedge is driven by the line end between the first two words quoted above which separates them like a defiant slogan from the following line which denounces them. The "wave," too, seems positive (and playful; "churned foam" becomes "wave," Hamlet is waving not drowning), however much the images foreground Hamlet's status as an actor, the human figure who bumps his head. Yet briefly in his space, he plays his part. "This moment and then, / that" acts out the space for the poet here. He is no longer dealing with the vast distances between his oppositions of gods and men, "Art" and life, but has found a text of cracks and spaces and broken surfaces, a precarious shelter.

Crichton Smith's poetry has been a poetry of discovery, a poetry which leads not to wholeness and completion but celebration of fragmentation. Thus when a poet who has made such discoveries writes a verse autobiography, he entitles it *A Life*, the indefinite article shrugging off definition and insisting that this is only one version. The dash at the end of the title of the last section, "Taynuilt 1982—" playfully and wilfully assumes significance here. In "The Survivors," "the hyphens, the dashes and the strokes" marked an exciting and yet dangerous incompletion. These lines point up the dash, signalling the incompletion of his own story of identity and marking a point of departure at which the poet is poised: a past behind him, a future ahead. The script is incomplete, the ending undecided. Yet it also invites the completion of a death date, deferred. Five sections precede the Taynuilt sequence: "Lewis, 1928-45," "Aberdeen University 1945-49," "National Service 1950-52," "Clydebank and Dumbarton 1952-55" and "Oban 1955-82." It is significant that identity, a life, is for the most part offered as a sequence of place names. "Who?" is read as "where?"

Lewis is, of course, the island "where was made the puritanical heart," the place of the dead, and of the past: "the rigid dead / sleep by the Braighe, tomb on separate tomb."[57] The rigid dead who claim the poet, however, are kept at a distance by "a" life lived on Lewis, and a shifting, changing and fluid identity created in poetry, the "I" for whom death lies outside language because the "I" is part of life alone, and can never know that he or she is dead, or as Bakhtin's pithy comment puts it, "In the cemeteries there are only others."[58] Lewis is the boy's home, the setting of the boy's relationship with his mother. This relationship is revisited and, as the mother lies dying, reversed, as mother becomes "my child, my child." Metaphors are revisited and rewritten, too. "Old Woman," a poem from *The Law and the Grace*, dealt sympathetically with the destructive elements of a personality formed by the island and her life there:

> Your thorned back
> heavily under the creel
> you steadily stamped the rising daffodil.[59]

The poet now inscribes that metaphor in a text of redemption, to be reclaimed only as metaphor, the aesthetic daffodil rewritten as a hardier annual:

> And the daffodils
> spring upward once again behind her heels.
> The hills are cardboard blue, the skies are red.[60]

Yet liberation is also loss. The woman is twice lost here; first in an historic sense and second in an aesthetic sense because "cardboard" and "red" somehow suggest a stage setting, defamiliarising the landscape so that we recognise its artificiality, the artificiality of a text which can no longer offer home.

The volume insists throughout on metaphors of the stage, of textuality, and the offering of different scripts. The form, a verse autobiography, prompts me towards comparison with "The Prelude," but the volume demonstrates throughout only its distance from Wordsworth. Where Wordsworth's "fair seed time" employs an organic image of wholeness and growth, Crichton Smith's image for his boyhood is one of dualism: "A winsome boyhood among glens and bens / casts, later, double images and shades."[61] To Wordsworth, "the bosom of the steady lake" offers a mirror-like reflection which reflects wholeness and unity."[62] To Crichton Smith, "double images and shades" offers a distorting glass in which self cannot be recognised. Awareness of disharmony, feelings of fragmentation, lead to the doubleness between man and actor and the feeling that he has been plunged into the wrong part in the wrong play. The scenario for Lewis is harsh and bare:

> Life without art, the minimum. I hear
> a sermon tolling, for your theatre is
> the fire of grace,
> hypothesis of hell, a judging face
> looming from storm towards boats and sea-drenched gear.[63]

The image of judgement seems to encompass the passage in "The Prelude" where the young boy borrows a boat and experiences a sense of self being judged as guilty. It also suggests the events of the *Iolaire* disaster, seen by Crichton Smith in terms of Greek tragedy. "Your" theatre rejects their script. His theatre, his own script, is the comedy of the cinema in Stornoway:

> Hardy, Laurel,
>
> plunged out of windows on their rubbery ladders
> in thin or baggy trousers. Errol Flynn
>
> wearing smoked glasses had the Japanese
> pilot in his sights.[64]

Rejecting the Lewis script of hell, damnation and judgement, he turns to the American film, the comedy where everything turns out right in the end, and a script which makes him not just a Lewisman, but a citizen of the world, encompassing America and Japan. The comic double of Laurel and Hardy, the "good" American guy and the "bad" Japanese enemy, offer images of self and other, and bring in the dualism of self. The faint allusion to the *Iolaire* disaster, however, shows that not yet confronted is the poet's anxiety about metaphor and society. The disaster was a real event with real consequences. The cinema screen springs into life as a metaphor which will bite back at him: art as a screen, a false stage set.

The first poem of the second section, "Aberdeen University 1945-49," offers the confrontation of a university-bound seventeen-year-old with a blind beggar in Aberdeen Railway Station. My impulse to invite comparison with Wordsworth and the encounter in Book Seven of "The Prelude" with the blind beggar, or with the leech gatherer in "Resolution and Independence," is thwarted as, once more, comparison reveals only difference. For Wordsworth, these encounters were inspirational. For the poet here, they reveal dislocation: "his definite shadow is the day's black stain. / How in such open weakness learn to live?"[65] "How" is only a moment of dislocation, forgotten by the poet scholar. Yet the song heard on the radio by the young poet lounging in the park, "Love O Careless Love," is the one Lowell hears, too, in this quotation from "Skunk Hour":

> a car radio bleats
> "Love O Careless Love. . . ." I hear
> my ill-spirit sob in each blood cell,
> as if my hand were at its throat. . . .
> I myself am hell
> nobody's here.[66]

And "I lie in Duthie Park with the *Aeneid*" surely suggests Lowell's "Falling Asleep Over The Aeneid." These allusions to Lowell perhaps introduce a sense of belatedness, of imitation. Like the chess game played by the major in the park, "a mimic and yet serious war," or the "transient images" of a nearby cinema, this life is an idyll, a rehearsal without consequence: "everything passes, everything is weighed / with a random music, heartbreakingly sweet."[67] The emphasis on "weighed" shows the poet using the line-end to give power to the word, a power deflected by the enjambment into "with a random music." In that gap is felt the power of the poet commenting on a younger self, acknowledging the innocence, the idyll, and the belatedness, too, and yet preserving the sweetness of those days, that life, which offers an individual who is at home with his books and learning, and who will never know such peace, such a sense of home, again.

National Service slams the door "shut on Milton and on Shakespeare."[68] The "random music" of Aberdeen becomes a different music, disciplined:

> We marched so beautifully, cleanly, then.
> It was a perfect music wrought from pain.
> EYES RIGHT.[69]

The poet is "we" here as "I tread / this glorious echoing stage" offers a self deprived of his individuality.

Crichton Smith was a teacher for thirty years. "Clydebank and Dumbarton 1952-55" offers a self in an environment which seems alien and hostile:

> Where is home?
> Not in this place with its tubercular bloom.
> The city is a painted yellow room
>
> for actors without dénouement.[70]

The image of the painted yellow room is a characteristic image of identity. Yet here yellow, the colour of psychological disturbance, is suddenly and firmly linked to Crichton Smith's fear of TB and death from that disease, finally making the base connection that has been rewritten in his poetry again and again as the irresolvable conflict between metaphor and society. To be "without dénouement" is to be imprisoned in a city of repetition and routine.

The "tubercular bloom" of Clydebank and Dumbarton is an image of infection. "Oban 1955-82" offers poems which more overtly use images of infection to reveal an identity and a script undermined and contaminated. The words which describe this process, "staining," "infection," "gnaw" and "unauthorised" fall into two distinct lexicons. The first two are from the lexicon of the disease TB, the symbol for the death of the man which is so difficult to write into the script. The second two concern that script and the way it is undermined by a "real" world around him. The authorised identity, the script, is constantly undermined by the breaking through of something which is unauthorised, which the poet has not written there. "Stain" and "staining" connect with an image of unweaving the tapestry of identity here:

> I constantly see the stain
> spreading on my calm jacket.
>
> I constantly see the braid
> unwind, unseam.[71]

The poet exploits a moment of poise at the end of each of the first lines of the stanzas quoted above: "stain" is held just that moment before it spreads, the "braid" identifies for just that moment before it disintegrates. Images from the two lexicons come together in a brilliant movement towards anarchy:

> The feathered quill
> is stained with red. The terrible
> agonised cry infects the page.[72]

The script is eroded by its opposite, enacting the violation of the poet's "world beyond this world" by the historical event of his mother's death. The poet who attempts to craft an identity is confronted by an unauthorised script, "unpredicted" and both feared and cherished. Oedipus's fate was to be claimed by his community, and here there is a similar sense of claiming and judgement. The teacher in Dumbarton inhabited a text without dénouement. The ending is now clear: the hero's dénouement is to be dethroned and pronounced guilty by his community:

Peasant that you are, realise
that you belong with them.
Your village is hideous

with the blood on the door
and your grass
is their grass.[73]

These poems offer a poetry of judgement on the tragic hero in images of an authorised text being constantly disrupted by something which he has omitted. In that collision, that disruption, is a script which forms the "real" I, the real poem: 'the sacred and abhorred / real poem has a waspish sting.'[74] It offers not a self created, but a self discovered, writable *and* already written, combining life and work. "The value of the vase is always paid" brings into his script the dénouement of *Oedipus Rex*, a terrible justice which is the uncovering of truth about self.

In 1987, Crichton Smith commented on the way his poetry has changed:

That flourishing . . . false to the realities of life for most people . . . didn't seem to correlate with the experiences of people, ordinary people, in a way. But now I think probably images . . . are part of what I do, the way I think.[75]

Linked in the quotation above are "ordinary people" and the "I" of Crichton Smith's poems. He is no longer set apart but suggests that he has managed to combine his art with his life. The title of *A Life*, then, with its division into places, shows an author situated in a real place at a real time, no longer rejecting the accident of geography and a hostile history. Like *Oedipus Rex*, Crichton Smith's poetry is a detective story whose dénouement is the discovery of self. *A Life* suggests an "I" who stands before a mirror which reflects not the legend of tragic heroes, but a completed, truthful self. No longer Prometheus or Hamlet, or Orpheus, he seems to offer direct address in the same kind of conscious turn Lowell took in *Life Studies*. Patrick Cosgrave's metaphor for this movement employs the image of stripping away foliage, an image which is prominent in Crichton Smith's work too, and which suggests an interesting parallel with Crichton Smith's stripping away of "shabby skins" in order to find out what is underneath.[76] Yet although Crichton Smith suggests a similar, conscious decision, the poems themselves show a text which crumbles, an unauthorised metamorphosis. The "silence" of the exile itself has been undermined.

In a comment on Lowell, Crichton Smith reveals a double movement of attraction towards and repulsion from a personal poetry:

Lowell at one stage was very personal, and then at the other stage becomes very public and his public poetry I think is not nearly so good as his personal poetry but it would be best if one could have the authenticity and intensity of the personal and also have something more objective into which it could be poured, if that could be possible. I think it's very difficult to do it nowadays with poetry because a lot of poetry now tends to be personal because of the lack of . . . an ideology.[77]

It is the desire for authenticity which draws Crichton Smith to a personal poetry: it is the desire for objectivity which demands heroes. The conflict between attraction and repulsion is revealed in a poetry which undercuts the metaphor of his text of heroes, yet does not wholly relinquish them, which strips the poet of his élitist identity but does so in images of attack, erosion, as something unauthorised, which offers *A Life* yet foregrounds the textuality, the arbitrariness of the reading. The writable and the already written merge in his work, and the identity is inscribed in neither. If the author is Crichton Smith, the man born in a certain place at a certain time, he is also a bundle of texts. It is textuality which can confront the death's head. The poet as text does not die: "the tale lives on." And the death of the man—that too can be turned into text. One of Crichton Smith's favourite books was *Oliver Twist* because "I seemed to identify with that waif of the streets setting out to find his identity."[78] Seeking identity in the mirror of his poems, he discovers a "waspish sting" because he uncovers an identity in which he is claimed by his society, and inscribed under the death's head. That inscription is rehearsed with the self as Oliver Twist in a text of traditional dénouement:

> So your death will be like a marriage,
> as a return of the lost boy
> to the house where he originally belonged,
>
> after he had been punished in an orphanage,
> forced to climb sooty chimneys,
> to put varnish on coffins.[79]

The hero of *My Last Duchess*, Mark Simmons, sees himself as "homo textual" and is tempted by the script of homecoming:

He would find her after many years and he would say, "I was wrong. I will do anything you wish. I will be whatever you wish me to be. I will no longer be the mental aristocrat, the aloof ridiculous backward man." Homo textual.

But as he looked into the varying patterns of the snow he knew that he had to come to the end of a certain road, that he had forced himself by some inner compulsion to the limits, that after all this was where he must have wanted to be, in the coldness of truth. Everyone got what they deserved in a way the Victorian novelists did not dream of.[80]

The Victorian novel, fat, rounded, complete, rejoiced in endings of marriage or death. But "the return of the lost boy" is a text that is refused by the poet. He has inscribed himself in a fragmented text. "Where he must have wanted to be" describes where the self is uncovered, a process of inner compulsion and discovery, a place of "varying patterns," and a point of no return.

In 1986, Crichton Smith commented:

I envy, for instance, those poets who have developed in a stable society, who can start from there and are not constantly analysing the very bases of their art.[81]

That analysis has produced a fine poetry, a poetry which is always questioned by the poet, a poetry in which language itself is always suspect. It has delivered the self created in the poems to a perpetual homelessness. It is a poetry which can yet inscribe self—and others. The last poem in A Life offers recognition and assigns position:

> The island, my vase, knows you.
> Your inscribed faces
> burn out of the brine:
> this is the sharp wine
> that educates us.[82]

Rather than graffiti, something scrawled across a text, violating it, the poet chooses here an image of etching. In this text, in this language, the "excised names of the exiles" can be read once more, the homeless finds his home.

The Village and Other Poems revisits Bourgeois Land two decades on. The temptation to see these poems as a homecoming, to write a return script for the poet, in terms of "a return of the lost boy," is overwhelming. Certainly there is a sense of joy about the poetry here, and compassion and understanding, which have always underpinned Crichton Smith's work, are foregrounded in a poetry where the poet writes with a sense of rediscovery, finding images of spontaneity and rebirth:

> At night
> I put out the ashes,
> and stand amazed
> beneath the blaze
> of a million million stars.[83]

Is this a poet at home in his world, at last finding grace, no longer sensing he has been born in the wrong place at the wrong time? Certainly there are images which suggest this. "A man is ploughing the land / with a red tractor" takes up the spectrum of colours Crichton Smith has developed and allows red, always the colour of the threat that comes with the flux and disorder of life, to be used in an image which suggests the preparation for new work, the promise of a rich new harvest.[84] Yet these images of homecoming and rootedness are undercut in several ways. In the opening sequence, poem 11 offers the image of the abandoned egg:

> It is a tiny earth among straw,
> cold now, without the throb of life in it.
>
> Who has touched it with his hands
> and left the smell of man on it?[85]

The images of infection and contamination which have permeated his work remain, then. Here this perfect creation, this world, lies abandoned and lifeless, suggesting the exhaustion of the old themes. Coupled with the image of death through the connecting image of the egg is "Incubator": this new life is "delicate as an egg in the machinery," the baby in harmony with machine, "till I grow tall, till I leave you / and seek soft human arms."[86] In many ways, Crichton Smith's personae have provided the machinery which has protected the poet, too, on his journey. Hamlet, Orpheus, Oedipus, have provided a framework which has allowed him to explore the personal, have allowed for the "authenticity and intensity of the personal . . . and something more objective into which it could be poured."[87] Here then, in *The Village and Other Poems,* we are promised the abandonment of the machinery, and the old themes, as part of a natural development. Such a development promises vulnerability and insists on the sense of precariousness. In "T.V." there is recognition of that development, seen as if in a backward glance, and awareness, too, of the inherent dangers:

The narratives overwhelm us, we need the white paper, unclouded,
we need in that furious hubbub a space for our names,
the sanity of prudent distance.[88]

Yet that space is no longer jealously protected. The poet urges himself to

> Put out your paintings:
> someone will notice them,
> even in the passing,
> in the wind of everyday.[89]

149

This is somehow art which exists and survives without the frame, without the separation of boundaries, art *in* the world. The last poem in the collection gathers up the themes of textuality and fabulation that permeate much of Crichton Smith's later work and sets up his position as narrator with the title "Listen." "Listen, I have flown through darkness towards joy" brings us through crises into the light again but also curiously brings us back full circle to the image of death contained in the cold green egg by allusion to the metaphor of life and death, the swift flight from dark, through the lighted corridor and into darkness again. It is a positive image, but a truthful one: death is written into the script. This new script allows surely for a new liberation, a new poetry. No longer is the poet pursuing a course which threatens to lead to silence. A new phase beckons:

> I had not believed that the stony heads
> would change to actors and actresses,
> and that the grooved armour of statues
> would rise and walk away
>
> into a resurrection of villages,
> townspeople, citizens, dead exiles,
> who sing with salt in their mouths,
> winged nightingales of brine.[90]

It is as if the poet has suddenly discovered himself freed from Bourgeois Land, and in another country, enchanted. Here Hamlet has been set free from his role and the tragedy of the solitary hero undergoes a metamorphosis: he discovers himself taking part in the comedy of existence within a community. Instead of a tragic soliloquy we are promised many voices "who sing with salt in their mouths." The conflict of the Gaelic inheritance has been resolved, absorbed into the poet's work.

In "Predestination," Crichton Smith explores the way in which the themes he has pursued, which seemed at the time spontaneous, gradually appeared to be part of a fixed pattern. In conversation in 1987, looking back on his published work, Crichton Smith commented that "what seemed to me to be a spontaneous book or a poem turns out to have been part of an overall fixed developing theme." At that moment, he turned to a page of *Thistles and Roses* and chose a verse from "Of A Rare Courage" to illustrate the discovery of "in spontaneous gestures a fixed fate." "Predestination" acknowledges that course: "The tram ran on rails. / My predestined stories."[91]

The publication of Crichton Smith's *Collected Poems* in 1992 offers the poems of forty years, and allows for exploration of the themes and patterns that are important in his work, and foregrounds the inevitability of the course, the courage and integrity of the poet who pursued it. The poems which close the collection are significant. "The Poet," first published in 1987, is worth quoting in full here:

> I have outdistanced the music
> I am travelling in silence
> through the shadow of posthumous metres
>
> What my metres will be
> will be what I shall become—
>
> I am the skin-made drum
>
> which the wind will fill.[92]

The imagery here offers a superb sense of freedom. To "outdistance the music" is surely to come to the end of the difficult and dangerous exploration of identity, to find that the "predestined stories" have been completed. It is not the freedom of exhaustion, however, but a freedom which promises new music, new poetry. And the past? What of the spectre of Calvinism that has haunted much of his work? That is no longer feared, no longer seen as destructive to his work. "If in this summer" promises that should these ghosts return, they will be inspirational:

> they would know the way through the old woods,
> and they would teach us
> how salmons climb thresholds.[93]

The poetry written from 1955-1992 offers a narrative which finally refuses the simplicities of the story of the prodigal son, finding in the position of disjunction and dislocation a poetry of delicate balance, which acknowledges both mirror and marble, and which speaks, not of endings, but new beginnings, and leaves the poet, once more, at the point of departure.

Notes

1. John Blackburn, "A Writer's Journey," booklet and five cassette recordings (Edinburgh: Moray House College of Education, 1981).
2. "Real People In A Real Place," in *Towards the Human* (Edinburgh: Macdonald, 1986), p. 30.
3. *The Exiles* (Manchester: Carcanet, 1984), p. 9.
4. *Ibid.*
5. "Chagall's Return," *Iain Crichton Smith: Selected Stories* (Manchester: Carcanet, 1990), p. 89.
6. *Towards the Human*, p. 21.

7. *Ibid.*, p. 35.
8. *Ibid.*, p. 21.
9. *The Exiles*, p. 20.
10. *Ibid.*, p. 10.
11. *Ibid.*
12. "From Scotland to Australia," *Scottish Review*, 19 (1980), 4-8 (p. 6).
13. *The Exiles*, p. 22.
14. *Ibid.*, p. 11.
15. *Ibid.*
16. *Ibid.*, p. 26.
17. *Towards the Human*, p. 26.
18. *Ibid.*, p. 54.
19. *Ibid.*, p. 21.
20. *Ibid.*, p. 27.
21. "The Highland Element In My English Work," *Scottish Literary Journal* 1977, 47-60 (p. 57).
22. *Ibid.*
23. Derick Thomson, *Why Gaelic Matters* (Edinburgh: An Comunn Gaidhealach, 1984), p. 26.
24. Iain Crichton Smith, *Selected Poems 1955-1980* (Edinburgh: Macdonald, 1981), p. 129.
25. "Writing in Gaelic," *Lines Review* 33, July 1970, 3-9 (p. 5).
26. *Collected Poems* (Manchester: Carcanet, 1992), p. 103.
27. Interview with Brian Hall, Aberdeen, May 12, 1986.
28. *Collected Poems*, p. 105.
29. *Ibid.*, p. 106.
30. *Ibid.*
31. *Ibid.*, pp. 103-104.
32. "Modern Gaelic Poetry," *Akros* 2:6, 1967, 27-41 (p. 41).
33. "A Meditation on Gaelic," *Chapman* 30, Summer 1981, p. 44.
34. *Collected Poems*, p. 175.
35. "A Meditation on Gaelic," *Chapman* 30, Summer, 1981, p. 45.
36. *Towards the Human*, p. 54.
37. *The Exiles*, p. 33.
38. *Towards the Human*, pp. 42-43.
39. *The Exiles*, p. 33.
40. *Towards the Human*, pp. 48-49.
41. Randy Barnes, "Seamus Heaney: An Interview," *Salmagundi*, 80, 1988, 4-21 (p. 21).
42. *The Exiles*, p. 46.
43. *Ibid.*
44. *Ibid.*, p. 47.
45. *Ibid.*
46. W. B. Yeats, "A General Introduction For My Work," *Modern Poets On Modern Poetry*, edited by James Scully (London: Fontana, 1966), 15-27 (p. 15).
47. *The Exiles*, p. 48.
48. *Ibid.*
49. *Ibid.*, p. 53.
50. *Ibid.*, p. 54.
51. *Ibid.*
52. *Ibid.*, p. 56.
53. *Ibid.*, p. 36.
54. *Ibid.*

55. *Ibid.*, p. 57.
56. *Ibid.*
57. *A Life* (Manchester: Carcanet, 1986), p. 9.
58. Tzvetan Todorov, *Mikhail Bakhtin: The Dialogical Principle*, translated by Wlad Godzich (Manchester: Manchester University Press, 1984), p. 98.
59. *The Law and the Grace* (London: Eyre & Spottiswoode, 1965), p. 16.
60. *A Life*, p. 10.
61. *Ibid.*
62. William Wordsworth, *The Prelude: or The Growth of a Poet's Mind*, edited by Ernest De Selincourt (London: Oxford University Press, 1926), V, 388, p. 157.
63. *A Life*, p. 11.
64. *Ibid.*, p. 16.
65. *Ibid.*, p. 19.
66. Robert Lowell, *Life Studies* (London: Faber & Faber, 1966), p. 62.
67. *A Life*, p. 21.
68. *Ibid.*, p. 27.
69. *Ibid.*, p. 29.
70. *Ibid.*, p. 35.
71. *Ibid.*, p. 43.
72. *Ibid.*
73. *Ibid.*, p. 44.
74. *Ibid.*, p. 48.
75. Interview with Iain Crichton Smith, Taynuilt, 1987.
76. Patrick Cosgrave, *The Public Poetry of Robert Lowell* (London: Gollancz, 1970), p. 110.
77. Taynuilt Interview.
78. "My Relationship With Poetry," *Chapman* 16, 4:4 (1976), 12-18 (p. 12).
79. *A Life*, p. 56.
80. *My Last Duchess* (London: Gollancz, 1971), p. 158.
81. *Towards the Human*, p. 51.
82. *A Life*, p. 64.
83. *The Village and Other Poems* (Manchester: Carcanet, 1989), p. 9.
84. *Ibid.*, p. 15.
85. *Ibid.*, p. 12.
86. *Ibid.*, p. 44.
87. Taynuilt Interview.
88. *The Village and Other Poems*, p. 54.
89. *Ibid.*, p. 35.
90. *Ibid.*, p. 69.
91. *Collected Poems*, p. 360.
92. *Ibid.*, p. 380.
93. *Ibid.*, p. 381.

Select Bibliography

VERSE

The Long River (Edinburgh: Macdonald, 1955)

The White Noon in *New Poets 1959*, with Karen Gershon and Christopher Levenson, ed. by Edwin Muir (London: Eyre & Spottiswoode, 1959)

Burn Is Aran [Bread and Water] (Glasgow: Gairm, 1960) includes short stories

Thistles and Roses (London: Eyre & Spottiswoode, 1961)

Deer On The High Hills (Edinburgh: Giles Gordon, 1962)

Biobuill Is Sanasan Reice [Bibles and Advertisements] (Glasgow: Gairm, 1965)

The Law and the Grace (London: Eyre & Spottiswoode, 1965)

Three Regional Voices, with Michael Longley and Barry Tebb (London: Poet & Printer, 1968)

At Helensburgh (Belfast: Queens University, 1968)

From Bourgeois Land (London: Gollancz, 1969)

Selected Poems (London: Gollancz, 1970)

Hamlet in Autumn (Edinburgh: Macdonald, 1972)

Love Poems and Elegies (London: Gollancz, 1972)

Penguin Modern Poets 21, with George Mackay Brown and Norman MacCaig (London: Penguin, 1972)

Eadar Fealla-Dha is Glaschu [Between Comedy and Glasgow] (Glasgow: University, 1974)

Orpheus and Other Poems (Preston: Akros, 1974)

Poems for Donalda (Belfast: Ulsterman, 1974)

The Notebooks of Robinson Crusoe (London: Gollancz, 1975)

The Permanent Island (Edinburgh: Macdonald, 1976), translations from *Biobuill Is Sanasan Reice* and *Eadar Fealla-Dha is Glaschu*

Nua-Bhardachd Ghaidhlig: Modern Scottish Gaelic Poems, with Sorley MacLean, George Campbell Hay, Derick Thomson and Donald MacAulay, ed. by Donald MacAulay (Edinburgh: Southside, 1976)

In The Middle (London: Gollancz, 1977)

Selected Poems 1955-80 ed. by Robin Fulton (Edinburgh: Macdonald, 1981)

Na h-Eilthirich [The Exiles] (Glasgow: University, 1983)

The Exiles (Manchester: Carcanet, 1984)

Selected Poems (Manchester: Carcanet, 1985)

A Life (Manchester: Carcanet, 1986)

An t-Eilean Agus an Cànan [The Island and the Language] (Glasgow: University, 1987)

The Village and Other Poems (Manchester: Carcanet, 1989)
Collected Poems (Manchester: Carcanet, 1992)

NOVELS

Consider The Lilies (London: Gollancz, 1968)
The Last Summer (London: Gollancz, 1969)
My Last Duchess (London: Gollancz, 1971)
Goodbye Mr Dixon (London: Gollancz, 1974)
An t-Aonaran [The Loner] (Glasgow: University, 1976)
An End to Autumn (London: Gollancz, 1978)
On The Island (London: Gollancz, 1979)
A Field Full of Folk (London: Gollancz, 1982)
The Search (London: Gollancz, 1983)
The Tenement (London: Gollancz, 1985)
In the Middle of the Wood (London: Gollancz, 1987)
Na Speuclairean Dubha [The Dark Glasses] (Glasgow: Gairm, 1989)
The Dream (London: Macmillan, 1990)

COLLECTED SHORT STORIES

An Dubh is an Gorm [The Black and the Blue] (Aberdeen: University, 1963)
Maighstirean is Ministearan [Masters and Ministers] (Inverness: Club Leabhar, 1970)
Survival Without Error and Other Stories (London: Gollancz, 1970)
The Black and the Red and Other Stories (London: Gollancz, 1973)
An T-Adhar Ameireaganach [American Sky] (Inverness: Club Leabhar, 1973)
The Village (Inverness: Club Leabhar, 1976)
The Hermit and Other Stories (London: Gollancz, 1977)
Am Bruadaraiche [The Dreamer] (Stornoway: Acair, 1980)
Murdo and Other Stories (London: Gollancz, 1981)
Mr Trill in Hades (London: Gollancz, 1984)
Selected Stories (Manchester: Carcanet, 1990)

COLLECTED ESSAYS

Towards the Human (Edinburgh: Macdonald, 1986)

Index

A Life 141, 146-148
"A Life" 124
"A Meditation on Gaelic" 133
"A Note On Puritans" 37
Aberdeen 17, 18, 83, 95, 143-144
"Aberdeen University 1945-49" 143
"Aberdeen" 84
"After Reading The Speech By The
    Rev Angus Smith . . ." 64
"After The War" 78, 80
Althusser, Louis 68
"Am Faigh A' Ghàidhlig Bàs?" 132
Anouilh, Jean
    Eurydice 93
Arendt, Hannah 58-59
"Argument" 88
"At the Sale" 62
Auden, W. H. 26-27, 103, 113
    "The Sea and the Mirror" 137
"Australia" 127

Bakhtin, Mikhail 9, 19, 142
Barthes, Roland 66
Bayble 9, 10, 14-17, 33
Beckett, Samuel 108, 114
Belsey, Catherine 68
"Ben Dòrain" 41-42
"Between Sea and Moor" 10, 14, 20, 31
Beveridge, Craig 25
Bibles and Advertisements 25
Bliadhna an Aomaidh 13
Bold, Alan 25
Brown, George Douglas
    The House With The Green Shutters 51
Bruce, George 32
Burns, Robert 26, 28, 53, 60-61, 66, 91
Buthlay, Kenneth 18
"By The Sea" 56

"Calling the Roll" 57
Calvinism 10, 13, 15, 17, 19, 26, 30-34,
    37-38, 51, 56, 59, 61, 64, 70, 78-82,
    85-86, 95, 100-102, 109, 113, 118, 137
Campbell, Ian 52, 56, 59, 68
Chagall, Marc 135
"Chagall's Return" 125

Cocteau, Jean
    Orphée 93
Consider The Lilies 37, 62, 82, 113
Cosgrave, Patrick 146
Crusoe 98-101, 103-110, 112, 114, 127

Dante 41, 52, 117-118
    The Divine Comedy 116
    The Inferno 116
    The Paradiso 116
"Deer On The High Hills" 26, 40-41,
    43, 47-48, 53
"Dido and Aeneas" 63
Dumbarton 26
Dunn, Douglas 137

Eichmann 58-59, 67, 70
Eliot, T. S.
    "Ash Wednesday, 1930" 135
    Four Quartets 14
"Envoi" 140
"Evening" 115

"Face of An Old Highland Woman" 17
"Farewell Party" 66
"For My Mother" 31, 83, 136
"For Poets Writing in English Over in
    Ireland" 137
Friday 106, 109
From Bourgeois Land 52, 54, 57-59, 64,
    67-68, 70
Fromm, Erich 59

Galair an t-srainger 11
Gibbon, Lewis Grassic
    Sunset Song 26, 29
Glasgow 9, 15, 25, 41, 64, 79, 81, 83-84
Goodbye Mr Dixon 104

"Hail Mary" 110
Hamlet 54-56, 58-60, 68-71, 77, 100, 103-105,
    108, 112, 123, 128, 141, 146, 149-150
"Hamlet in Autumn" 68
Heaney, Seamus 136

Helensburgh 26
Holbein, Hans 89
  The Ambassadors 77
Homer 117-118

Iain Am Measg Nan Reultan 131
"If in this summer" 151
In The Middle 68, 98, 109-110, 114-116,
  118, 124
"In The Middle" 115
In The Middle Of The Wood 108, 116
"In The Surgery" 111
"Incubator" 149
Iolaire 12, 78, 81, 88, 143
"Iolaire" 78, 80
"It Was A Country" 29

Kailyard 51-54, 56-57, 59, 68, 70
Kant, Immanuel 43
Kay, Billy 26, 29
Kelly, Ned 128
Kierkegaard, Sören 54, 55, 58

Lacan, Jacques 19
Laing, R. D. 25
Larkin, Philip 137
Lewis 9-15, 17, 18, 26-31, 33-34, 37, 47,
  61, 70, 79, 81-82, 95, 98-102, 104, 108,
  113, 117-118, 143
"Listen" 150
*Little Red Riding Hood and An Dorus
  Iarùinn* 131
"Love if you are love" 92
Love Poems and Elegies 78, 81, 83, 85,
  92, 98-99, 114
Lowell, Robert 78, 147
  "A Quaker Graveyard in Nantucket"
    78
  "Falling Asleep Over The Aeneid"
    144
  Life Studies 146
  "Skunk Hour" 144

MacAulay, Donald
  "A Delicate Balance" 123-124
MacDiarmid, Hugh 25-28, 41-42, 47, 53,
  112, 114, 132
  "A Drunk Man Looks At The
    Thistle" 59

"Consummation" 92
"On A Raised Beach" 42, 47
"The Watergaw" 41
"To Circumjack Cencrastus" 27
Macdonald, Finlay J. 16, 17
Macintyre, Duncan Ban 41-42, 45-46
Macintyre, Lorn 31
MacLean, Sorley 101, 130
"Meditation Addressed to Hugh
  MacDiarmid" 27
Merrill, Thomas 110
Morgan, Edwin 67
My Last Duchess 20, 68, 147

Nicolson Institute 17
"No-one at home" 91

Odysseus 128-129, 134
Oedipus 123-124, 130, 138, 145-146, 149
"Old Highland Woman Reading
  Newspaper" 33-34
"Old Woman" 32, 34, 38, 142
Oliver Twist 147
"On Helensburgh Sea Front" 28
On The Island 10
Orpheus 93-96, 98, 101, 103-105, 112,
  123, 128, 146, 149
"Orpheus" 92, 93

"Painting The Walls" 113
Petrarchan 92
Plato 89
"Poem of Lewis" 20, 29
"Predestination" 150
"Prepare Ye The Way of The Lord"
  110, 111
Prometheus 112, 146
"Prometheus" 29
Prospero 101, 137

"Remembering" 117
"Resolution and Independence" 143
"Resurrection" 92
"Retiral" 67
"Return to Lewis" 131
"Returning Exile" 124
Rilke, Rainer Maria
  "Orpheus, Eurydice and Hermes" 93

Ross, William 29
"Rythm" 36

Saltire Review 78
Sartre, Jean-Paul 108
"Schoolgirl On Speech Day" 34
"Schoolroom Incident" 36
"Schoolteacher" 33-34, 36
"Scotland" 56
Scott, Alexander 18
Selden, Raman 66
Selected Poems 1955-1980 132
Shakespeare, William 116
Shklovsky, Victor 45
Smith, Christina 9-10, 71, 77, 81
Smith, Gregory 25
Smith, John 9-10, 81
Sophocles 123
"Speaker" 64
"Speech for a Woman" 125-126, 134-135
"Speech For Prospero" 137
"Statement By A Responsible Spinster" 33, 55
Stevens, Wallace 86
Stornoway 10, 17, 81, 143
Stornoway Gazette 12, 80
Stuart, Prince Charles Edward 128-129, 130
"Studies in Power" 37
"Sunday Morning Walk" 38-39, 42, 113, 114

"T.V." 149
Tawney, R. H. 59
TB 11, 12, 30, 56, 70, 81, 85, 145
"That Island Formed You" 84
"The 'Ordinary' People" 139
"The Black Jar" 113
"The chair in which you've sat" 89
"The Critic and the Poem" 113
"The Dedicated Spirits" 26
"The dream" 91
"The Elite" 112
The Exiles 124
"The fever" 92
"The Iolaire" 78, 80
The Last Summer 10-11, 16, 19, 63, 67, 82
The Law and the Grace 25, 30, 142
"The Law and The Grace" 60
"The Legend" 139

The Long River 26, 28, 44, 47-48, 53, 57, 86, 87
The Notebooks of Robinson Crusoe 98, 109, 115, 124, 130
"The Notebooks of Robinson Crusoe" 98
"The Poet" 151
"The Purple Bucket" 113
"The Scholar" 114
"The Space Ship" 85
"The Survivors" 139, 141
"The Temptation" 52, 53
The Village and Other Poems 148-149
"The White Air of March" 56-58
The White Noon 30, 102
"The Widow" 33
"The wind roars" 52
"The Witches" 34
"There Is No Sorrow" 126
"This clutch of grapes" 87
Thistles and Roses 25, 30, 35, 52, 62, 140, 150
Thomson, Derick 14, 16, 18, 132
    Why Gaelic Matters 131
"Those Who Move Others" 116
"Three Sonnets" 38
Tiresias 18, 138
"Today I Wished To Write A Story" 103
Turnbull, Ronnie 25

Virgil 63, 64, 117, 118

"When They Reached The New Land" 126
"Whether Beyond the Stormy Hebrides" 53
"Who Daily" 139
Williams, Tennessee
    Orpheus Descending 93
Wittgenstein, Ludwig 103, 105
Wordsworth, William 113
    "The Prelude" 142-143

Yeats, W. B. 138, 139
    "Easter 1916" 136
"You are at the bottom of my mind" 134
"You told me once" 85
"You'll Take A Bath" 134-136, 138
"Young Highland Girl Studying Poetry" 35